# FIND YOUR OWN SINGING VOICE

**VOCAL TRAINING FROM FUNDAMENTALS TO MASTERY, TECHNIQUES TO HELP YOU ENJOY SINGING MORE AND MORE**

STEPHEN GREENLANE

# CONTENTS

# INTRODUCTION

"It is a tale that you sing. As long as you
believe it, it makes you powerful."
—Kieron Gillen

**Enthusiasm is a key ingredient in good singing.**

To sing is one of the oldest and most fundamental needs in a human being's life. It can heal, it can console, and it can rejoice. It can tell a story or put feelings into sound in a way nothing else can.

So many people deny themselves the joy of singing because they believe their voices would make listeners cringe. "You're either born with the talent or not," is often said.

While it is undoubtedly true that some individuals are born with an innate ability to sing like angels, anyone can sing. All you need is the willingness to learn and practice and eventually step out of your comfort zone.

This ebook will equip you with all the theoretical knowledge and practical exercises needed to put you on the road to singing freedom. While most terms are explained within the chapters, a short glossary is also included at the end for your convenience.

Experience the profound personal growth and a deep sense of accomplishment, of feeling 'whole' again, that comes with singing.

# HOW MY SINGING CAREER STARTED

I am a self-taught music teacher and performer with many years of experience. My journey with singing started at the age of 12, and I honed my skills by performing all kinds of songs.

I am deeply passionate about singing and believe practice deepens the experience. I spent years researching both the theoretical and practical aspects of singing and have concluded that music is infinite.

I wish to share my knowledge and experience to help other enthusiasts get better at their art and experience the deep satisfaction of understanding its nitty-gritties.

My singing career started by accident. I was told to perform in a skit on a day's notice since the lead singer had backed out at the last minute. Like any novice who doesn't know a cent's worth of anything about music, let alone singing, I freaked out. Since I knew I would screw up, I didn't pay much attention to how bad I was. Instead, I used the time on my hands to mimic a lullaby I remembered from my childhood. This helped me gain confidence to sing the next day.

When I performed, I realized that I wasn't as bad as I thought I was. I didn't rock the stage, but I didn't blow it either. The fact that, despite being untrained and inexperienced, I was able to sing intrigued me so much that I went on to explore singing for the rest of my life.

Singing is an art, and like all things, it can be mastered with time and perseverance.

# A BRIEF WALK THROUGH HISTORY

Everything has roots, and singing is no different. The vocal production of singing sounds predates any spoken language we know in history. Ancient people sang their thoughts before they spoke them. It is generally accepted that the first communications were more like bird songs and the roar of animals (Koopman, 2019).

Vocal traditions were probably influenced by the speech patterns that evolved in specific regions, although it has not been proven yet. It may not be a coincidence that the Italian vocal technique called bel canto (meaning beautiful singing) developed in a country known for open, easy vowel sounds. Modern French singers have a distinct timbre only found in French-speaking countries.

The oldest notated piece of music dates from 800 BCE, showing that the Sumerian civilization already distinguished singing as an art form from religious or folk music.

The Roman Catholic church dominated the music scene from the fourth century CE for the next 13 centuries. Singing styles evolved during this time from plainchant to highly complicated harmonious patterns, such as those found in the music of Palestrina.

The prevalent musical style changed from polyphonic to homophonic in the Baroque era (1600–1750).

The influence of the group of humanists, musicians, poets, and intellectuals in Florence, Italy, who became known as the Florentine Camerata, facilitated the emergence of theatrical music as we know it today in the late 1500s. It was near the end of the Renaissance period, and music moved from the reverberant environment of religious sites to theaters. Singers learned to combine singing with movements, and the musical accompaniment started developing into an element in its own right.

## Contemporary Styles

Our idea of what constitutes good singing has changed dramatically over the past decades. Anything goes, from Céline Dion-style belting to 'whisper pop,' a breathy, soft style favored by many modern artists. The focus has shifted to tone and storytelling—it may be going full circle again through history.

Whatever your style is, you can do it well and enjoy it immensely.

Anyone can sing!

# YOUR VOCAL CORDS: THEIR PLACE IN SINGING

Your vocal cords produce the magic that is your singing voice. They are folds of tissue that stretch across the top of the trachea (windpipe) and vibrate when air moves over them.

The vocal cords, the cartilage, and the muscles supporting them form the larynx.

## CORDS OR FOLDS?

Some experts have ditched the traditional name of vocal cords in favor of vocal folds. A cord conjures up an image of a string plucked, but vocal folds don't function like strings (Weill Cornell Sean Parker Institute for the Voice, 2019).

They form part of a muscle on the side of the larynx, and their outer covering of specialized tissue is the only part that vibrates in moving air.

# HEALTHY VOCAL FOLD FUNCTIONS

The biological function of the vocal cords or folds is to protect the lungs and airway. The two strings of the ligament are located at the point where the esophagus and the airway separate. They open to allow breathing but close during swallowing to prevent food from entering the lungs.

They are surrounded by muscles called the thyroarytenoids that attach to the thyroid. The muscle can be called the TA for short.

When air from the lungs is blown against the cords while they are in an almost closed position, the outer folds vibrate to produce sound. The air is pushed through a small slit between the cords with enough force to make the vocal coverings, known as the mucosa, vibrate.

This process is called the venturi effect in scientific terms. Whenever air or fluid is squeezed through a constriction (venturi), it creates low pressure, leaving a suction effect in its wake.

The suction draws the pliable folds of the mucosa together, only for them to be pushed apart again by more air coming up from the lungs. The cycle of movement created is known as the mucosal wave. A regular mucosa wave is essential to produce good quality sound.

There is a great free video to watch on YouTube at **https://www. youtube.com/watch?v=g4JBeKvFhz8** that shows how the movement happens (Weill Cornell Sean Parker Institute for the Voice, 2016). The folds move more than 100 times per second, but the photography was slowed down through a stroboscope, and the wave can be observed clearly.

The folds are supported by a specialized gelatinous band of collagen called Reinke's layer. Adequate elasticity in this layer is essential for good voice production and singing stamina.

The pressure of the air determines the loudness of the voice pushed through the vocal folds. A forceful explosion produces a louder sound. Tension in the vocal folds must be increased to maintain the half-closed position necessary for the venturi effect. If the folds and supporting structures are not strong and pliable enough to do this, the air will push them apart, and vibration will be lost.

The frequency at which the mucosal wave occurs determines the pitch of the voice. The folds are also able to lengthen and shorten, besides vibrating. That helps to regulate the tension, which alters the pitch.

In the lower registers, the TA muscles are responsible for pitch. Another group of muscles comes into the picture in the higher registers called the cricothyroid muscles (CT for short).

The CTs pull the cords somewhat forward and down, while the TAs just increase or decrease the tension while the cords are short and thick during the singing of low notes. The actions of the CTs make the cords longer and thinner to sing high notes. It is similar to stretching a rubber band.

## THE IMPORTANCE OF MUSCLE STRENGTH

Instead of wood, strings, and steel, a singer's instrument comprises muscles, ligaments, and tissues. The vocal cords are only the size of an adult's thumbnail, but they can produce three or more octaves of sound.

This is made possible by the interactions between the muscles, ligaments, and tissues. The strength and flexibility of the TA and CT muscles have to be balanced to produce good sound, where training and practice come in. Just like you train your other muscles in workouts in a gym, the muscles around the vocal folds have to be trained and strengthened to improve your singing.

Too much TA tension will make it difficult to reach high pitches, while relaxing the TAs too much will make the stretching effect of the CTs strong enough to shift your voice into falsetto.

This tug-of-war between the two groups of muscles will balance out through exercises. The TA muscles are usually more active in beginner singers, making it difficult to sing high notes. In more advanced singers, warmups before a performance or lesson relax the TAs enough to allow the CTs to engage properly.

Many singers struggle with the switchover between the two muscle groups. It occurs between the lower and higher register, and if not done seamlessly, it causes the voice to crack, grow faint, and struggle. Lightening your singing style when you approach your break will make it easier. The spot where you experience your transition break will be different from the next person's, and some exercises will be more effective for you than others.

We'll explore the transition in more detail in the next section.

## THE DREADED BREAK IN THE VOICE

The point where you transition from one register into the other is popularly known as the break in your voice. Some singers have used a marked break as a trademark, some even creating a yodeling effect.

The intentional break is often used to signify emotions such as surrender or devotion, going from a metallic-sounding note to a much softer high pitch. Céline Dion uses this to great effect in the timeless classic song "The Prayer." Other singers who favor an intentional break include Alanis Morissette, KD Lang, and Michael Jackson.

An unintentional break is a different story, however. It is viewed as undesirable in good singing technique, and inexperienced singers are taught to maintain their singing mode when moving into a different register.

As your vocal experience grows, you will learn when to expect the transition and be ready for it.

Register breaks occur when the larynx stays static in the position utilized in the previous register. The soft palate, tongue, and breath control also play a role.

It mostly happens when transitioning between the chest and head registers, both up and down. Trying to carry the chest register too far up will result in a clumsy attempt by the laryngeal muscles to compensate, leading to the break.

## Belting

The belting technique carries the chest register singing mode as high as possible to infuse the sound with force and energy. While the 'pushed' sound may enhance some contemporary music to add emotion or create a dramatic effect, it cannot permanently be used as the primary singing style without damaging the vocal folds. The singer will not experience any voice development either.

It can be very difficult for singers who are used to having this over-energetic, heavy, and dark quality to their voices to learn proper vocal technique and obtain a healthy mix of the registers. They often fear losing what they perceive as the power in their voices when they allow laryngeal muscle control to change.

That will be quite noticeable in the beginning when singing in the middle and high registers using the correct technique. For instance, they will struggle to sing soft ballads because their voices will be shaky, wavering, and thin. It might sound like a boy going through puberty's voice changes.

Don't be scared of the sound and despair that you have lost your voice. The reason for the awkward voice is the underdevelopment of the muscle group supporting the head voice and the overdevelopment of the muscle group supporting the lower registers.

Muscle development is a gradual process, and you as a vocal student have to trust what will happen naturally to your voice when you sing correctly. With patient practice (guided by a knowledgeable coach if possible), your voice will grow and strengthen, and your bout with a thin, shaky voice will soon be something of the past. The sound that will eventually emerge will be so rich and true that you will be amazed.

Suppose you wish to return to some measure of belting for effect in your music. In that case, you have to keep singing lighter in your exercises to avoid falling back into the same problematic registration pattern.

There are a couple of points that belters can keep in mind while working to ditch their old habits and create new ones:

- Work on increasing the vocal cavity in its totality.
- Pay attention to your singing posture.
- Switch to your head voice earlier in your middle register during exercises.
- Sing softer in your middle and upper registers until you have mastered the new technique. That will help you resist the temptation to push because belting needs volume.
- Start your exercises high and go down rather than the other way round.

## Tensing Up

Do you tense up, consciously or subconsciously, when you know the break is coming? If you grow tense, you activate a squeezing reflex that narrows the vocal tract and causes the larynx to rise. A telltale sign of this type of tension is bulging muscles on the side of the neck. The constriction can cause a slightly off-pitch tone.

This pattern usually develops over time and can be stubborn to shift. The best advice to overcome this is to take it gradually. Don't go too far up in your exercises but stay in a comfortable mid-range, just entering the danger zone. Concentrate on staying relaxed and keeping your resonance cavities open. Even if you only sing one note into your higher register, that note has to sound free and open. When you have mastered the first note, add the next until you can transition freely into your upper register.

## Lowering the Soft Palate

For some singers, their primary problem with breaks is going down from the middle register to the chest voice. They tend to lower their soft palates as they get to the breaking point. That pushes the sound into the nasal cavity, producing a thin, somewhat nasal sound that is not consistent with the rest of the singer's voice.

The nasal resonance cavity favors thinner, brighter sounds because it is smaller and cannot accommodate the formants that give body and color to the voice.

## Retracting the Tongue

A common mechanism often employed subconsciously to try and regulate the larynx during transitions is to retract and flatten the tongue. The tongue bunches up in the back of the throat and sits heavily on the voice box, thereby inhibiting the larynx even more.

That increases the chances for a disastrous break and makes it difficult to reach higher notes.

The voice quality produced will be very dark and sound uncomfortable and gagged.

Sit in front of a mirror and sing the vowel 'a.' Observe the behavior of your tongue. Do you pull it back?

Next, speak the vowel and watch what your tongue does. Sustain your speaking voice into an extended 'aaa' while maintaining that tongue position. Speaking and singing are not that different, after all! Vary the pitches and keep practicing until you have mastered them.

If you're not sure what it feels like to have your throat unobstructed, try singing a note with the tip of your tongue resting on your lower lip. While that tongue position is too far forward to ever use in singing, it will teach you what feeling to go for.

## Regulating the Airflow

Too much pressure from airflow is a common cause of disastrous breaks. That can result from tensing up because of performance issues or bad habits, and constant belting can cause it.

The right amount of air pressure is crucial to the behavior of the vocal tract. To help you find the sweet spot, sing through a couple of repetitions of a rapid scale on a 'z' or 'v' sound. You might find that your usual break didn't appear and that your head voice was instantly brighter and stronger.

# "NOT FOR ME, I SING MODERN STUFF"

Do I hear you say this talk about breaks and balanced voices is for classical singers only? You might be surprised how much a balanced, mixed voice will benefit your contemporary music.

The contemporary sound will be stronger without shouting, and the occasional light belting will be even more powerful. During belting sessions, listeners will get an impression of a huge range still available to the singer instead of feeling that note could barely be reached.

That will make it easier to add the special touches that bring individuality to the performance because singers don't have to worry about their voices deserting them at critical moments.

# EXERCISES TO MIX REGISTERS

These exercises don't need to be performed loudly. Female singers should take extra care when switching between the mezzo and contralto sections of their voices, while males should pay attention to the transition between their falsetto (the highest) voice and head voice.

## The Reversed Siren

The sound of a siren usually goes up, but for this exercise, the sound must go down from the highest note you can reach to the lowest. It will be similar to yawning while making a high-pitched sound and ending in a low sigh.

Take care not to force your voice, especially before you have warmed up properly, but let the sound flow freely and naturally to glide through the breakpoints.

Take the slide slowly and if you notice a crack or 'jump' in your voice, take the next slide even slower at that point until you can do it evenly.

## Messa Di Voce

*Messa di Voce* is Italian for "placement of the voice." The exercise requires you to pick a vowel sound ('la' is the easiest to start with) and sing it on a comfortable pitch.

Start the note softly, swell the sound in a crescendo, and slowly move into a decrescendo before letting it trail away in silence. Throughout the note, the placement of your tongue, soft palate, and lips have to remain the same, and your sound quality has to remain constant. The only variable will be your volume.

## Singing Octaves

This exercise is the flip side of the siren. Instead of gliding up an octave (eight notes), you must jump cleanly from the bottom to the top or vice versa.

Start with a note just above or below the point where your voice usually breaks. Take care to hit the note an octave higher or lower without scooping to it. You have to hit the pitch with confidence and a clean sound.

## Trills

When executing trills, the voice is placed exactly where it should be in terms of the balance between muscle groups. Trills promote relaxation, and learning to move from the trill position to a vowel in the same position will establish correct muscular patterns without any pushing or obstructing.

Trilling with the lips or tongue tip on the neutral sound 'uh' (as in 'good') opens the throat. The pressure is concentrated at the lips or tongue, teaching you how little pressure you need on your larynx to produce a certain pitch.

Switch from a trill on a certain pitch to a vowel on the same pitch to establish the right placement.

# THE ANATOMY OF THE VOICE

## CHAPTER 2

A scene from Rossini's opera *The Barber of Seville* in the DuPage Theater in Lombard, Illinois. The historic building has since been destroyed.

Singing is not magic or simply a born talent, but an art that can be learned by understanding its basics and practicing diligently, regardless of the style you favor.

In this chapter, the fundamentals of voice anatomy and the role of different body parts in producing sound will be discussed in more detail.

If you've ever been flummoxed by advice such as "keep your voice strong," "sing from your diaphragm," or "support," keep reading! Although singing is a science, it turns out it's not rocket science, after all. Your efforts will play a significant role in determining the kind of singer you will become.

With practice, acts like voice placement and breathing will become second nature to you, and you won't have to concentrate on them consciously any longer.

# THE FUNDAMENTALS OF BREATHING

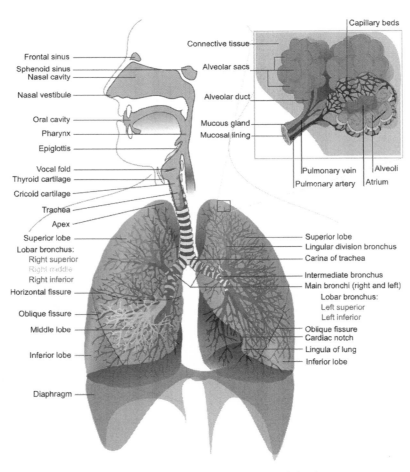

A detailed diagram showing the airways and diaphragm.

You won't reach your full potential as a singer if you don't become aware of your breathing. It may be something you do without giving it another thought in everyday activities, but when you sing, the picture changes.

The basic breathing mechanism starts with chemical signals from the brain that the body needs oxygen. That causes the diaphragm, the big muscle under the lungs, to contract. The contraction moves the diaphragm downward, creating a vacuum in the lungs, increasing their capacity. The air pulled in through the nose rushes to fill the vacuum.

Once the lungs are full of air, the diaphragm relaxes again and pushes upward. That decreases the lung capacity, and the air is forced out.

## The Diaphragm

The diaphragm is a thin muscle that separates the abdomen from the chest cavity. It is dome-shaped, with the right side slightly higher than the left.

The center tendon is anchored by muscular fibers extending from the lumbar spine, sternum (breastbone), and bottom of the rib cage.

The heart is also attached to the diaphragm via the pericardium, the membrane that envelops the heart. During breathing, the heart moves up and down with the diaphragm.

Besides breathing, the diaphragm helps to create essential pressure in the abdomen to push out substances such as feces or vomit. A strong diaphragm can also help reduce acid reflux, the bane of many singers' existence, by putting pressure on the esophagus.

## The Lungs

Looking like inverted trees, the two spongy, elastic organs are big enough to take up most of the space in the chest cavity. Air enters the lungs via the trachea. The trachea branches into two bronchi, where it enters the lungs.

The bronchi keep on branching into smaller bronchioles. A small cluster of sacs called alveoli is located at the end of each bronchiole, where the oxygen-carbon dioxide exchange occurs.

Every human being has hundreds of millions of alveoli in their lungs.

A thin lining, the pleura, covers the lungs to help keep them elastic and separate them from the chest wall. An infection of the pleura called pleurisy causes sharp chest pains when breathing, and it can be disastrous for a singer. It is best to treat a cold or flu before getting out of hand.

## Abdominal and Back Muscles

Whenever you're told to support your voice, these are the muscles that come into play. The most important of these are called the intercostal muscles.

This group of muscles is found between the ribs. They facilitate the expansion and contraction of the rib cage during breathing.

Proper, deep diaphragmatic breathing gives an excellent workout to these muscles to strengthen them. It is common for new vocal students to tire quickly and start struggling to breathe deeply and correctly.

Of the abdominal muscles, a couple is important in breathing. The transverse abdominals are a broadsheet of muscles on the front and sides of the abdominal wall. It is considered an essential part of what Pilates instructors call the core.

The pair of external obliques are the largest of the abdominal muscles. They make up the outer wall of the abdomen.

Between the transverse abdominals and the external obliques are the internal obliques.

All of these muscles have to work with the diaphragm for effective breathing.

The pair of quadratus lumborum muscles in the lower back stretch from the lowest rib to the top of the pelvis.

The large pair of psoas major muscles are connected to the diaphragm and run from the lumbar spine to the groin, where they join the femur, passing in front of the hip joint.

## SUPPORTING YOUR VOICE

In simplified terms, your voice is supported when you contract your abdominal muscles to create higher pressure in the thorax and abdomen. That makes it possible to control the movements of the diaphragm to regulate and slow down the amount of air leaving the lungs. A controlled release of breath sustains the voice in terms of pitch, volume, and vibrato far better than a quick exhalation can.

Novice singers or older people who grow too weak to support properly often have a noticeable wobbly quality to their voices.

We'll dedicate a later section to specific techniques to strengthen your support.

## HOW IS SOUND PRODUCED?

At its most basic level, the sound is produced by moving air. When air is exhaled from the lungs through the throat and larynx, the vocal folds vibrate or buzz, and the sound emitted is shaped by the lips, tongue, palate, and other articulators.

- Sounds like 'm' and 'n' are made by allowing air to enter the nasal cavity above and behind the nose.
- Bilabial sounds like 'b' and 'p' are formed when the lips are pressed together, and the air is forced out in a small explosion.
- When the teeth touch the lower lip, sounds like 'f,' known as labiodental sounds, are produced.
- Dental sounds like 'th' are formed by pressing the tip of the tongue against the upper teeth.

Intonation or variances in pitch are achieved by varying the amount of air coming through the opening between the vocal folds called the glottis.

# RESONANCE

Tuning forks are good demonstrations of vibration
and resonance-producing sound.

The vibration in the larynx causes the surrounding structures to start vibrating or resonating, too.

Other body parts that can resonate in harmony with the airflow that produces the voice include the chest, mouth, throat, face, nasal cavity, sinus cavities, and skull.

What is known in vocal technique as placement concerns the part of the body resonating with the voice during a particular note.

# FORMANTS

The sound produced by the vocal folds does not consist of one single tone. There is a base frequency and several overtones called formants. Together, the lowest frequency and the multiples of overtones form the harmonic series of the speaking or singing voice. They can be heard in vowels.

If a spectrogram of a voice is taken, the formants show up as peaks in the graph.

Formants will be explored deeper later in the ebook.

# PHONATION

The term refers to the system of producing sound through the larynx, which is then modified through articulators.

It takes time to master the intricacies of phonation and make any adjustments. Knowledge of the anatomy of sound organs can make the process easier for singers.

# ARTICULATION

Your style of articulation and the effective use of articulating components play an important role in good singing. You can't tell a story with your song if the audience can't hear what you're singing.

The controlled passage and vibration of air through the articulators shape the words. Some articulators can move, such as the mouth, lips, jaw, facial muscles, soft palate, and tongue, while others such as the teeth and dental plate are fixed.

# BREATHING TECHNIQUES FOR SINGING

As explained before, your breath plays a vital role in determining the quality of your singing. To become good at singing, you need to learn to control your breath by understanding different breathing techniques and their uses.

In this chapter, you'll get to know different breathing techniques to help you improve your voice control. Knowing which techniques will help you and which could harm your voice is essential because not everybody who purports to understand vocal coaching knows the correct and natural ways to breathe.

Be kind and gentle with yourself and take it slow. You don't have to master singing excruciatingly long phrases in one day. Build your muscular strength and lung endurance slowly.

## GET BREATH FEEDBACK

Monitor the position of your breathing by placing your hands under your lowest rib with your thumbs pointing backward. Breathe in and check if your diaphragm section is moving up.

This area between the bottom of the sternum and the navel, extending sideways to the lower ribs, is known as the epigastric region.

Your hands should move in and out noticeably while you breathe. Otherwise, you are not properly utilizing your support.

Don't force your abdomen, stomach, or any other part of that region to expand, as that will create tension in the lower back and produce the opposite effect. The ribs will move inward instead of out, the sternum will fall, and lung volume will decrease instead of increase. It can result in unnatural phonation.

During a lesson or performance, you can place your hand on your upper abdomen as a reminder to breathe properly and deeply.

This way of breathing will tire your intercostal muscles because they will work much harder than during talking.

## SILENT BREATHING

When performing, breaths have to be taken silently, and this has to be practiced. If you struggle to get it right, try inhaling through your nose before singing a note.

Nose breathing slows down the amount of air that can be inhaled in one breath and positions the larynx, vocal tract, and abdominal muscles in the best configuration for good sound production.

## "BREATHING OUT THE VOICE"

This technique will help you understand how your body supports your breath, regardless of the sound being made.

Inhale and then exhale on an 'ahhh' sound for two to three seconds. Allow your voice to trail away and exhale the last air on just a whoosh.

Become aware of how the whole exercise happens on one continuous breath.

# THE FARINELLI MANEUVER

Learning to slow down the pace at which breath is used during singing is useful to gain full control over the voice, especially on high notes and during long passages. The Farinelli maneuver involves keeping the diaphragm, lower ribs, and belly distended during exhalation as if inhalation continues.

- Inhale to the count of four.
- Hold completely still for a count of four. Don't push in any way to hold your breath because that will create tension in your abdomen and larynx.
- Gently release the breath to the count of four.

Practice holding your breath for longer until you can comfortably reach 10 seconds in, 10 seconds hold, and 10 seconds to exhale. Never wait so long that you have to gasp for air. The breath expulsions and renewals must be relaxed, controlled, and quiet.

This is an excellent way to learn to pace your breath. It is important to work out how much air is needed for a passage during the practice of the piece and to be able to take in and sustain adequate air to sing it well.

You can practice the Farinelli maneuver with sound by singing parts of a scale in a comfortable range. Take in the air, sing a couple of quarter notes, then take in a silent breath in the time another quarter note would have taken before singing the rest.

Gradually move on to a line or two of your favorite songs, practicing this technique.

# AN EASY BREATH CONTROL EXERCISE

An enjoyable way to master breath control is to practice the well-known song "Amazing Grace." The song is no longer copyrighted, being published before 1922 in the US, and can be reproduced safely here (Music Services, Inc., 2021).

The lyrics of this song are familiar to most of us, and the chances are that you have always sung it, taking breaths at specific places without even thinking about it.

You are now going to sing it more legato, taking fewer breaths and creating a flowing sound that is true to the story that is being told.

Read the words of the first five bars: "Amazing grace, how sweet the sound...." Are you perhaps used to singing the first two words, then breaking off to take a breath, and then singing the rest?

Although there is a comma after the word 'grace,' the whole phrase is a unit meant to be sung in one breath.

Now you try to sing the first phrase without breaking. Don't go loud, and don't think about interpretation. Just take a deep breath and sing through the phrase without rushing it.

**The melody line of Amazing Grace.**

If you did not succeed at first, don't despair. Keep trying—I promise you, it gets easier! One day you will suddenly realize that your brain has taught itself to release your breath in a controlled way, long enough to sustain the phrase. That happens because you communicated a meaningful unit to your brain to work with, and our brains love seeing the reasons behind actions.

The song has to be divided into only four phrases in terms of breathing. When you feel up to it in your control, you can make a slight pause after the words followed by commas without breathing in.

# COMMON EXERCISES TO AVOID

Some exercises that have become common over the years can do more damage than good to your technique and voice, or at best, just waste your time without adding value.

## The Book on the Chest

Lying down on your back with a heavy book on your chest while you breathe is one exercise in the latter category. The idea is that correct diaphragm breathing will move the book up and down, and you will be able to see if you do it correctly.

While this looks impressive, it doesn't help much. It only gets you used to the feeling of the weight before you breathe correctly. Rather practice proper breathing in a normal performance situation such as standing to ensure it becomes second nature to you quickly.

## Staccato Breathing

Another popular exercise is staccato breathing. Students are told to take in as much air as possible and release it in three sharp, rapid, explosive breaths. The teacher checks that the diaphragm jumps up during the explosive expulsions to ensure the student makes air noises coming out the mouth.

It can benefit if this exercise is used sparingly as a sort of "diaphragm crunch" to strengthen the muscles. It has no use in learning correct breathing techniques, however. Singers don't expel their breath explosively during a song. This also goes against the controlled, relaxed breathing pattern required for good voice production. Forceful breathing also impacts the vibrato of the voice negatively.

## Belly Breathing

The term belly breathing is often used interchangeably with diaphragm breathing, but it is not the same.

Diaphragmatic breathing involves only the epigastric region, while belly breathing refers to the whole abdominal cavity, down to the pelvis.

Some teachers tell their students to breathe down their whole hypogastric area, including the lower abdominals and pelvis. The test for this type of breathing is to see the stomach moving up and down, and students are encouraged to put their hands below their navels. Exhalation is usually fairly forceful.

Belly breathing comes from the German tradition of singing and is known in the literature as *Bauchaussenstutz*.

It should be clear by now that this is incorrect from an anatomical point of view. The diaphragm is not located low in the abdomen, and no amount of forceful inhalation will stretch it lower to expand the air capacity.

Thrusting out the stomach only creates muscular tension where it is not helpful. The accompanying forceful exhalation also creates high pressure in the glottis that could damage the vocal folds because they are blown apart.

# CHEST BREATHING

Some singers allow their shoulders and clavicles to move up during inhalation. It is also known as shallow or exhausted breathing. That is the way we pant after exertion when we just want to get some air into our lungs as quickly as possible.

It is counterproductive for singing because the lower parts of the lungs never fill with air when we breathe this way. The sternum collapses, and the support muscles can't do their job properly either.

Chest breathing also tends to be quite noisy.

Avoid letting the rib cage collapse completely at the end of every phrase to minimize the temptation to breathe in the chest. Keep your upper body upright and your rib cage expanded.

# INHALING TOO DEEPLY

In an attempt to "stock up" on air for the coming phrases, some singers keep taking in air, regardless of the phrase they need to sing right after that breath. It often results in noisy gasps and air running out on crucial points in the phrase.

Trying to inhale too deeply over a period can bring on hyperventilation and dizziness, ruining your performance.

# ACHIEVING POISE IN YOUR VOICE

Poise is all about control, and control in singing is about breathing. This chapter will take breathing a step further and explore how you can use it to hone your voice to be a fine instrument fit for a master at the craft of singing.

We'll take a look at the essential elements for achieving poise.

## STRENGTHEN YOUR CORE

Strong core muscles and a good posture will improve your breathing, which will, without doubt, improve your sound. An upright posture will ensure you have the greatest possible chest cavity available to breathe and for the sound to resonate in.

The chest should be kept high to give the diaphragm free movement. It will also help release tension and improve airflow through the vocal folds, enabling you to sustain longer notes.

What does a good singing posture look like?

- Stand up straight and keep your body relaxed.
- Make sure your shoulders are relaxed, not bunched up around your ears or pulled back.

- Keep your feet shoulder-width apart.
- Tilt your weight slightly forward, and don't lock your knees.
- Keep your chin parallel to the ground.
- Keep your chest elevated and open.

If any part of your body feels uncomfortable in your position, change it. You have to be in a posture that enables you to sing the best you can.

# SUPPORT FROM YOUR DIAPHRAGM

It can't be emphasized enough how important it is to support your voice and breathing from your diaphragm. Besides regularly exercising your breathing technique whenever and wherever you think about it, you could also use a balloon to help you strengthen this important muscle.

## The Balloon Exercise

- Lie down on your back, bend your knees, and put your feet up. If you're lying on the floor, use a chair to prop your feet up.
- Hold the balloon in one hand and rest the other hand on the floor next to you.
- If your back allows you to raise your buttocks without you getting hurt in any way, raise yourself about two inches up from the floor.
- Take a deep breath through your nose and blow all the air into the balloon.
- Relax your shoulders and neck so that your diaphragm and midsection will do the most work.
- When you've exhaled fully, wait about five seconds before inhaling again.
- Press your tongue against the roof of your mouth while breathing in.

- Keep doing this until the balloon is fully blown up.
- Rest for a few seconds and go again—see if you can repeat the exercise five times.

## All-Fours Breathing

Another simple exercise to strengthen your diaphragm involves getting down on your hands and knees.

- Make sure your hands are under your shoulders and your knees are under your hips.
- Round your back slightly, as if you are doing the cat pose in yoga.
- Inhale through your nose and exhale through your mouth.
- Round your back even more while you breathe out and tuck your chin in toward your chest.
- Wait for five seconds before inhaling again.
- Repeat the exercise five times.

## The Hissing Exercise

This exercise aims to let your breath out in a controlled manner, as softly and slowly as possible. It is especially helpful when singing low notes because it strengthens the feeling of abdominal support you need to sing full-voiced at a low pitch.

- Hold your hand above your navel to make sure you use the right region and inhale through your nose.
- Close your teeth and open your lips slightly.
- Keep your tongue touching your bottom teeth.
- Exhale slowly on a soft 'tsss' sound.
- Try to sustain the exhalation for 30 seconds.
- Repeat the exercise five times before resting.

## Diaphragm Problems

Several medical conditions can cause diaphragm problems, and if you experience pain while exercising, breathing, or singing, you should get yourself checked out by a doctor.

Strenuous exercise can cause a spasm known as a side stitch. If you feel this type of sharp pain while doing your singing exercises, it might be better to hold off for a few days so the muscle can rest.

A hiatal hernia happens when the top of the stomach pushes up through the opening in the diaphragm into your chest cavity. It can be extremely painful and could need surgical repair.

The most important nerve running through the diaphragm, the phrenic nerve, sometimes gets infected and swollen due to disease or trauma to the midsection. The nerve is crucial in respiration, and one of the main symptoms is unexplained, chronic shortness of breath. It is a serious condition and should be treated by a medical professional right away.

General symptoms of impaired diaphragm health include heartburn, silent acid reflux, chronic coughing without a cold or flu present, difficulty swallowing, chest pain, bluish skin due to an oxygen shortage, headaches, persistent hiccups, pain under the lower ribs, and a fluttering sensation under the ribs.

## Tips for a Healthy Diaphragm

- Eat frequent, small meals.
- Chew thoroughly.
- Avoid foods that cause heartburn for you.
- Sleep with your head slightly elevated if you are prone to silent acid reflux during the night.
- Keep a healthy weight.
- Before starting strenuous breathing exercises, do a few stretches and bends to warm up your diaphragm.

# LUNG HEALTH

The importance of healthy lungs for a singer needs no explanation. There are a couple of things you can do to keep them in tiptop condition and expand their air capacity.

First and foremost, if you are a smoker, STOP! You are not doing your breathing or your voice a favor by smoking. Even secondhand smoke can damage your respiratory tract and vocal cords.

It is not always possible to choose or control the quality of the air you breathe, but if you have a choice, go for the best. Use indoor air filters if you live in a dusty area. Invest in a humidifier if your residence is in a dry climate. Reduce irritating pollutants such as artificial fragrances, chemicals, dust, and mold to the minimum.

Keep any vaccinations you might need and flu injections up to date.

Make sure you eat enough food containing antioxidants. Antioxidants help prevent inflammation, such as flu and pneumonia, and reduce the chances of allergies, such as asthma, developing.

- Apples, beets, peppers, pumpkin, turmeric, blueberries, tomatoes, red cabbage, green tea, olive oil, yogurt, oysters, Brazil nuts, Swiss chard, coffee, barley, anchovies, cocoa, and lentils are all known for their high antioxidant content.

# EXERCISES TO STRENGTHEN YOUR CORE

A strong core will bring body and voice in balance with each other and give you more stamina for sustained high-quality vocal delivery.

Suppose you struggle to support well enough or long enough, have chronic low back pain without injuries or illnesses, feel like it's a huge effort to produce the voice, or struggle with persistent tension in the jaw, throat, neck, and shoulders. In that case, it might be time to give your core muscles some loving attention.

## What Is the Core, Exactly?

From the neck to the places where the arms and legs join the torso, the whole trunk is known as the functional reflexive core (FRC). This area has the biggest influence on the quality and stamina of our voices.

The FRC has two layers. The inner consists of the throat, diaphragm, transverse abdominal muscles, psoas muscles, and pelvic floor muscles. The outer layer comprises all the other muscles that form part of the torso.

Although stability in the outer layer is important, the voice needs strength and flexibility in the inner layer. General body tension, breathing, and movement all influence this layer.

Our modern, sedentary lifestyles condition us to move less than we should. That can lead to stiffness and difficulty breathing deeply. Our backs can grow weak and rounded, making it difficult to keep the chest cavity open.

The prevailing opinion of fashion and body image that only flat abs are acceptable causes us to suck in our abdominals permanently. That hampers the functionality in the midsection of the body greatly. If you experience engaging your support almost like bracing before a punch in the stomach, the chances are good that your abs have forgotten how to do their jobs properly.

You can easily test the level of tension in your abdominal muscles by lying on your back with your knees bent and your feet flat on the floor. Put your hand on your belly, close to your belly button, and cough five or six times. If your stomach pushes up into your hand when you cough, you carry too much residual tension in that area.

## Easy Exercises to Start You Off

To condition the FRC, you have to think holistically and not isolate muscles. Concentrate on decreasing the general level of your everyday tension and breathing calmer and deeper.

Stand on all fours on the floor or a yoga mat and let your belly hang loosely toward the ground without hollowing your back. Keep your pelvis relaxed. Breathe normally and focus on feeling your abdomen loosening with each breath. Stay in that position for about five minutes, if you can.

If you try to sing a phrase or two in this position, you might notice interesting reactions from your body that show you where you are still carrying too much tension.

To wake up the inner layer of the FRC, you have to reverse positions. Lie flat on your back with your knees bent and your feet on the floor. Support your head on a low pillow so your rib cage can touch the floor. Keep your pelvis relaxed to keep some space beneath your lower back.

Place one hand on your midsection and one on your lower belly. Breathe in and see which section moves the most. Ideally, it should be the area around the ribs. Exhale slowly on a hissing sound. Feel your core becoming active halfway through the exhalation without trying to pull your navel down toward your spine.

Do the exercise five to seven times in a row. Don't lose heart if you don't feel your core engaging initially. With repetition, those muscles will wake up.

Take the previous exercise a step further by doing the following: when you get halfway through exhaling, lift one foot slowly off the ground so your leg is bent at a 90-degree angle and feel your FRC engaging. Keep your leg in this position while you inhale again and lower your foot on the next exhalation. Repeat the exercise with the other leg.

One side of your body might find this movement easier than the other. Notice if your hips wobble when you lift your leg or if your back flattens. That will indicate some weakness that has to be exercised.

## THE IMPORTANCE OF WARMING UP

Now that you know your vocal folds are muscles covered with tissue capable of vibration, you can understand the importance of warming up these muscles before using them strenuously.

You wouldn't dream of going to the gym for a workout and grabbing the heaviest weight on the floor as soon as you walk in, without stretching and warming up first. Why do it to your voice?

The overall better shape your voice is in, the shorter the time needed for warmup will be. Still, even a singer like Luciano Pavarotti religiously warmed up before every practice and performance. Just look at Pavarotti vocalizing in full costume and makeup before a performance of Aida in this Youtube video: **https://www.youtube.com/watch?v=kuiqJ5IeXsA** (George's Opera World, 2020).

Another useful analogy is to compare your vocal cords to a rubber band. When the band is warm, it is elastic, soft, and stretches far without breaking. However, it is brittle and hard when it is cold and breaks easily.

Warming up doesn't need to be complex. There are simple but extremely effective routines.

A few things to keep in mind when you start your warmups:

- Start gently and softly—never force your voice into a note or volume that feels uncomfortable at that point.
- Focus on your breathing during warmup while you don't need to concentrate on performance.
- You don't need to keep warming up for coaching or performing days only. Twenty minutes of a simple warmup every day will help you in the long run. Arpeggios are great for daily exercises. (An arpeggio consists of the different notes of a chord sung in rising or descending order.)
- Never tilt your head backward while singing or warming up because that puts unnecessary strain on your vocal folds.
- Remember to stay hydrated. Your vocal folds need plenty of fluids to remain supple. Dry vocal folds cause the notes to crack and mucus to form as protection.
- Do not hydrate with cold fluids just before a performance—rather stick to something warm and soothing such as herbal tea; rosemary and mint work quite well. Cold liquids can make even

the tiniest amount of mucus hanging around sticky enough to ruin a note. The tea should not be hot either because that will cause your mucus membranes to swell.

- Do a couple of head rolls to loosen your neck and throat; bend sideways and forward with your arms swinging loose to get rid of tension around your diaphragm.
- Pull your shoulders up as high as you can and let them fall a couple of times.
- Challenge your range during your warmup routine. If it doesn't work, it doesn't matter.

## Vowels

One of the tried and true methods is to sing all the different vowels in arpeggios. Try to do one sequence of a vowel (all the notes in the chord) in one breath.

You can also sing your arpeggios staccato (short notes, not gliding). That helps with the pitch and placement of the voice.

## Humming

Humming gives you an excellent start because it does not strain the vocal cords. Keep your mouth closed and move up and down the scale on a 'hmmm' sound. Include 'h' to minimize strain. Relax your tongue by keeping the tip against the backs of your bottom front teeth.

## Lip Trill

The lip trill, or lip buzz as some people call it, involves sounding like a motorboat with your lips half-closed. Your lips should vibrate while the air moves through your mouth and nose.

Slide up and down any pitches that are comfortable to you.

## Tongue Trill

This one can be tricky for some people, don't worry if you can't manage to do it. Curl your tongue and make an 'rrr' sound while sliding up and down the scale as a playing toddler does.

## Loosening the Jaw

A flexible jaw that can open wider while singing than speaking is important for good sound production, especially on high notes. Loosen your jaw muscles by pretending to yawn.

Take care not to drop your chin merely. Place your finger in the hollow under your jaw that is in line with your earlobe, and make sure you feel your jaw moving there when you open your mouth.

## Pitch Glide

Work on the breaking point between your chest and head voice by gently gliding up and down two octaves on a comfortable vowel sound such as 'ahhh' or 'ieee.' Try not to change the feeling of where the sound is produced during the whole glide.

## Jump and Portamento

In Italian, the portamento exercise is called portamento della voce, meaning to carry the voice. It is almost like the siren exercise but slightly more consciously sung.

Choose an easy vowel like 'ahhh' and start on a comfortable pitch. Jump an octave higher, sustain the note for four counts and slide down the notes again until you get to the same one you started on. Go up (or down) a halftone and do the same until you reach your voice's limit.

Remember to support the sustained note.

## Tongue Twisters

Getting your tongue around a difficult phrase isn't just for kids. It's great for singers, too. It loosens your tongue and lips and gets you in the right mode for clear diction.

Try "a proper cup of coffee from a proper copper coffee pot" or "a synonym for cinnamon is a cinnamon synonym" on any tune you like.

## SOVT Exercises

SOVT exercises, or semi-occluded vocal tract exercises, are done with the mouth partially closed. The pressure reflected from the lips helps the vocal folds vibrate more easily.

It is simple to do SOVT exercises—just put a straw in your mouth and sing like you normally would. You can pretend your lips are now located at the end of the straw if that makes it easier.

No air should escape around the straw from your lips or through your nose. Singing on a 'b' sound works well.

If you don't have a straw handy, you can also use a paper cup. Punch a hole in the bottom with a pen and seal the top edges of the cup around your mouth.

If there's neither a pen nor a cup on hand, singing on a nasal 'nggg' or 'mmm' can help out to get the back pressure effect.

SOVT exercises are especially helpful when you detect a breathy quality in your voice that you didn't create intentionally as part of your style or if you struggle to sing legato/smoothly.

When you have a busy day of rehearsals, performances, or recordings, doing a few rounds of SOVT exercises can be a lifesaver to counter voice fatigue.

# FINDING YOUR UNIQUE VOICE

Your unique voice type is the quality that defines your sound. When you utilize the strong points of your voice type, there will be no stopping you. On the other hand, working against your voice type will exhaust you and potentially damage your vocal tract irreparably.

The 'color' of your unique voice is your stamp of individuality. It'll help you find your unique singing personality and develop your own singing style and vocal playlist.

## THE FACH SYSTEM

Finding your voice type involves more than just determining your vocal range. The German classification system known as the Fach system recognizes 25 different voice types based on various criteria.

The system was started in the late 1800s to help opera singers find suitable repertoire for their voices in auditions and productions. After singers had their voices classified in a category, they could study with a teacher in that same Fach (voice category).

According to Fach, composers wrote their operas with specific sounding voices in mind, and casting ensured an authentic production was presented.

There are ten variables to consider when deciding on your voice type.

# Range

Although the range is not the most important factor, it is crucial. A soprano cannot sing the bass notes without straining her voice and vice versa.

Female singers' three main range types are soprano, mezzo-soprano, and contralto. For males, the ranges are tenor, baritone, and bass. We'll get to a detailed description of each a bit later in this chapter.

# Tessitura

The notes in your range that you feel the most comfortable singing and have the richest sound is where your voice's tessitura is.

The Italian word tessitura means 'texture' and refers to your sound's unique texture.

# Transition

We have discussed the break in the voice between the chest and head voice earlier. Technically it is known as the transition point between the lower and higher register.

The exact notes where the transition occurs vary between voice types.

# Register

The number of high notes in your high register and the number of low notes in your low register are also related to the type of voice you have.

Some voices have a balanced number of each, while others tend to have more of the one than the other.

## Weight

Don't worry. This has nothing to do with your weight on the bathroom scale. It is the weight of your voice, meaning whether your voice sounds heavy and dark or bright and light.

If we relate this factor to well-known contemporary singers, Adele has a dark, sultry voice, while Taylor Swift has a much lighter quality to her voice. Both sing beautifully, but they are very different from each other.

In the opera world, we have Placido Domingo with his rich, dark tenor voice, while tenor Juan Diego Florez has a much lighter sound. Both are outstandingly successful professional singers, but they go for different roles in the same opera.

## Size

This refers to more than volume. Some good singers sing loud enough to fill a concert hall right to the back, but their voices sound almost one-dimensional. Others may not sing so loud, but their voices seem to come alive with drama.

## Talking Voice

The normal pitch at which they speak indicates their voice type in most people.

It can be misleading, though. Consider the mezzo-soprano Katherine Jenkins, for example. Her voice is much lighter when she talks than when she sings.

## Timbre

This quality refers to what is known as the color of a voice. The distinct mixture of basic frequencies and overtones gives a specific voice its character and sound.

The concept will be explored more fully later in the ebook.

## Experience and Age

Your singing experience and your physical age will influence your voice type. Vocal cords don't mature fully until the late teens and early twenties. Men have their voices breaking, but women do, too, even if it is to a much lesser extent.

As female singers age, they tend to get a deeper, darker voice quality. This gets more pronounced in experienced singers.

## Physical Qualities

Your weight, height, and build play a role in the quality of your singing voice.

# FEMALE VOICE TYPES

Within the three main categories, there are various subtypes. We'll take a look at each of them.

## Soprano

The highest female voice type has a range that stretches approximately from middle C to the second A above. Sopranos can be subdivided into five categories.

### Lyric Coloratura

These ladies can easily reach incredibly high notes, and their voices are bright without being shrill, crisp, and agile. Their music contains many trills, runs, and leaps.

Think the *Queen of the Night*-aria with its top F-notes here or the music of the South Korean pop sensation of the mid-1980s, Kimera.

### Dramatic Coloratura

While the notes in this voice category are still very high, the voice quality is darker, somewhat warmer, and usually unbelievably powerful. Their voices are just as flexible as the lyric coloraturas' because they sing the same range of notes, although they sound different.

Maria Callas and Joan Sutherland were two of the greatest opera names in this category.

### Lyric Soprano

They have the same bright quality as the coloratura sopranos, but their top range ends slightly lower. It is the most common female voice type.

Light lyric sopranos sound young and sweet even when they are older, while full lyric sopranos sound more mature.

Examples of well-known full lyric sopranos are Reneé Fleming, Kiri te Kanawa, and Anna Netrebko. A contemporary light lyric soprano is Mariah Carey. Céline Dion falls in the full lyric category.

### Dramatic Soprano

Rich, deep, and colorful tones are characteristic of this Fach. They evoke emotions from their listeners with a dark timbre, and their tessitura is lower than the other sopranos'. Their voices tend to be extremely powerful. They have slightly thicker vocal folds than the other sopranos, so their vocal delivery might not be as agile as the higher sopranos, but the sound is full, and the quality is sustained.

In operas, they usually sing tragic, heroic roles. They are also often associated with Wagner operas. The American soul icon Patti Labelle is a good example of contemporary music.

### Character Soprano

Their voices are good mixes of the qualities of all the other categories.

## Mezzo-Soprano

It is often said that mezzos have the best of both worlds. Their range extends into both the high and low register. It usually stretches from the A below middle C to the second F or G above middle C.

The main difference between sopranos and mezzo-sopranos lies in their tessituras. The mezzo voice's most beautiful and rich-sounding part is lower than a soprano's.

### Coloratura Mezzo-Soprano

The coloratura mezzo-soprano can reach fairly high notes like in the soprano category. Their tone is bright, warm, and rich, and their voices are flexible. Their agile, high registers are comparable with most sopranos, but the distinction lies in the warmth of their lower registers.

An excellent example of this type is the highly versatile opera voice of Cecilia Bartoli. The American opera singer Joyce DiDonato also falls into this category.

Pop music does not make such clear distinctions as in classical singing, but Beyoncé is clearly in the coloratura category with a range of four octaves.

### Lyric Mezzo-Soprano

With the characteristic mezzo warmth but lacking the agile, high register of the coloraturas, lyric mezzos are best known for trouser roles in opera. They are young male characters that require a lighter voice than a man's.

The lyric mezzo voice cannot reach the same volume as other mezzo-sopranos. Their sound is sensitive and smooth, and although they can sound melancholy at times, they are always easy to listen to.

The Irish pop singer Enya is a good representative of this voice type. With a reported range of almost five octaves, the late great Whitney Houston was also an outstanding lyric mezzo-soprano.

In opera, the names of Dame Janet Baker and Elina Garança spring to mind.

## Dramatic Mezzo-Soprano

The most impressive voice type in the mezzo-soprano Fach is the dramatic. Their voices are incredibly big, warm, and rich. They can sing over a big orchestra and chorus easily, filling opera halls right to the back without sound-boosting equipment. On occasion, they have been described as "lyric mezzos on steroids" (Jonithm, 2015).

Their medium registers are the strongest. Their upper registers are still warmer than those of sopranos, while their lower registers border on those of contraltos.

For a practical illustration of the power and versatility of a true dramatic mezzo, watch this 1962 video made of Maria Callas singing the aria "O don fatale" from Verdi's *Don Carlo*: **https://www.youtube.com/watch?v=Mvlc8-Ni4QM** (NDR Elbphilharmonie Orchester, 2021).

Note the abrupt changes from low to high register that Callas handles without batting an eyelid. The recitative ends on a high B-note, morphs into a cantabile melody in the middle to low register, and finishes in a prolonged ending that climaxes on a high B-flat note.

Dolora Zajick is a perfect example of the dramatic mezzo among modern opera singers.

In contemporary music, the powerful sound of Adele qualifies as dramatic mezzo.

# Contralto

The lowest female voice is the contralto. They are also called altos, although the terms are not interchangeable, technically speaking. Alto refers to a specific choral part in a very specific voice range.

Their voices extend far into the low register and have a dark, smoky character. Their middle registers tend to be short compared to other voice types, and they don't struggle to attain crescendos in the midrange.

## Coloratura Contralto

Coloratura Contralto is the rarest of the low female voices. It is lighter than the other two and more agile, able to sing intricate, florid passages in operas such as those Rossini composed.

The Polish-born Ewa Podleś, with her exceptional range of more than three octaves, stretching from the baritone B-flat to the soprano high D, embodies the epitome of agility. She is equally successful at contemporary music and Baroque works.

## Lyric Contralto

Lyric contraltos are the most common of the low female voice types. Their voices are also light, but they are not as agile as the coloraturas. Their lower registers extend just as far as the other contraltos without sounding equally dark.

The easy-listening voice of Karen Carpenter from the 1970s brother-and-sister duo The Carpenters falls into this category.

Gilbert and Sullivan favored lyric contraltos in operatic repertoire for many of their roles, such as Little Buttercup in *H.M.S. Pinafore*.

## Dramatic Contralto

The darkest, deepest, most powerful, and heaviest female voice is the dramatic contralto.

According to some experts at the Metropolitan in New York, they are fairly rare and have been getting even more difficult to find as time goes by. "If teachers are urging voices upward, and contraltos are being billed as mezzos, simple economics may have something to do with it" (Myers, 1996). Their repertoire is extremely limited because of the rare and heavy quality of this Fach. There are few opera roles written especially for them, and they tend to be cast as singers mainly of music by composers such as Mahler and Handel. The operas where they feature are mostly German pieces such as Wagner's. That could make it difficult for a true contralto to pay the rent every month.

It is, however, a beautiful voice quality, and those who possess it should cultivate and nurture it.

Cher, Joan Armatrading, and Tracy Chapman are contemporary singers who have this voice type.

# MALE VOICE TYPES

Male voices can also be divided into categories and sub-categories, some of which are similar to the female categories.

## Tenor

Probably the best known among the male singers are the tenors. If an opera cast could be compared to an orchestra, the tenors would be the trumpets with their clear, ringing voices.

They are considered the highest male voice in the modal register, and their typical range stretches from C3 to G4.

The Italian word *tenere* means "to hold," and in early music, the tenors held the melody line. They were the driving force in the performance, so to speak, guiding the other voices in terms of tempo and pitch.

Many modern pop singers are tenors, although contemporary styles often disguise the true pitch of their high notes. It is only when you try to sing along that you find out exactly how high these guys can go. An example is Sir Paul McCartney's voice in The Beatles' songs.

### High Tenor/Countertenor/Contra Tenor

These guys are the male counterparts of coloratura sopranos. Their voices are extremely agile, and their falsettos are unbelievably strong and beautiful. The clear ringing sound of a well-trained countertenor can challenge and surpass many sopranos.

The voice type is rare, especially in modern music. Bruno Mars is one contemporary example of a countertenor in pop music.

The opera roles that countertenors typically sing were originally written for singers called castrati. They were young men who were castrated before their voices could break, so they retained their light, high voices. The practice started in Europe in the mid-16th century.

The castration and accompanying lack of testosterone prevented their bones from hardening as they should have. They grew out of proportion and had exceptionally large rib cages. That enlarged their lung capacity, and they could hold a note much longer than other singers. That ability, combined with golden voices, delighted audiences, and they became the stars of the opera stages in the 17th and 18th centuries.

After Italy's unification in 1861, castration was declared an illegal operation. At the beginning of the 1900s, the Catholic Church banned the hiring of castrati and decreed that boy sopranos had to be used in church music.

The last castrato who sang in the Sistine Chapel choir was Alessandro Moreschi. A 1902 recording of his voice survived. While it is very different from the sound we have become accustomed to from modern singers, it is still a remarkable piece of music history. You can listen to it on Youtube at **https://www.youtube.com/watch?v=KLjvfqnD0ws** (Medina, 2021).

Famous countertenors include people like Andreas Scholl, Philippe Jaroussky, and David Hansen in modern times.

### Lyric Tenor

They typically have light, warm voices that sound soft but are quite powerful.

Most of the famous tenors we remember are lyric tenors. Think about people like Enrico Caruso, Beniamino Gigli, Luciano Pavarotti, and Juan Diego Flórez.

In more modern music, the names of Freddie Mercury and Michael Jackson immediately come to mind.

### Dramatic Tenor

While their voices are also extremely powerful, and they eat top Cs for breakfast, the color of dramatic tenors' voices is generally darker than those of lyric tenors. While lyric tenors can have "dark moments" in their voices, depending on the pitch and content of what they're singing, the darker timbre is sustained in dramatic tenors, regardless of the pitch.

Tenors who alternate between dark and light sounds are sometimes classified as spinto tenors. The pop singer Chris Brown is a good example of a spinto.

Dramatic tenors are also known as "tenore di forza" or "robusto" because of their clarion-like, forceful delivery. Some sound close to a baritone but can sing higher notes than baritones.

Plácido Domingo, Jose Carreras, and René Kollo are well-known dramatic tenors in the opera world. Bryan Adams, Billy Joel, and Ed Sheeran are dramatic pop tenors.

## Baritone

Baritones occupy the middle range of male voices. Their sound is warm, laid-back, and easy to listen to. Timeless great names like Roger Whittaker and Bing Crosby belong to this Fach. Their smooth middle registers are more suited to country-western and R&B songs than pop music, where tenors are favored.

The term 'baritone' comes from the Greek word βαρύτονος, which means 'deep-sounding.'

The baritone range usually falls between G2 and E4.

In operas, they usually play the role of the tenor's love rival or his best friend, an older hero, or a seductive older man.

Baritone David Serero.

## Lyric Baritone

The lighter, less harsh version of the baritone sound is called lyric baritone. Their tessitura is somewhat higher than for the other baritones.

Frank Sinatra, Nat King Cole, Michael Bublé, and John Legend are excellent examples of this voice type. Dietrich Fischer-Dieskau and Gerald Finley made their mark in opera as lyric baritones.

## Dramatic Baritone/Verdi Baritone

This is where voices like those of Bing Crosby, Johnny Cash, Elvis Presley, and Barry White really come into their own. Some of them, such as Elvis, could double as a tenor, while singers like Barry White and Bing Crosby could easily reach bass notes.

On the opera stage, the world still mourns the passing of the great Dmitri Hvorostovsky. One of the most beautiful voices of yesteryear is Titta Ruffo.

## Bass-Baritone

Males with this voice type have extensive and impressive registers, straddling the baritone and bass ranges.

An excellent bass-baritone in recitals, as well as operas, is Sir Bryn Terfel. Other names include Simon Estes and José van Dam.

Joe Cocker, Louis Armstrong, and Don Williams can be classified as bass-baritones in contemporary music.

# Bass

The lowest male voice with its velvety rumble is the bass. Their usual singing ranges are from F2 to E4. The low C is their equivalent of the tenors' and sopranos' high C.

Finding a pure bass is a rare occurrence—many low baritones sound like basses and can do much of the bass repertoire with ease. A genuine bass has a tessitura between G2 and A3. Some music writers estimate that only about five percent of all bass singers can be classified as true basses (Gemtracks, 2021).

The human ear struggles much more to detect low frequencies than higher ones, and it takes a lot of skill and a very special type of voice to make these magnificent low notes sound so clear and brilliant over an orchestra.

Unlike tenors or sopranos that are quite typecast in opera roles, basses can portray either villains or wise, old men. Opera composers also used their unique voice qualities to portray characters that were not of this world, such as devils and gods.

### Lyric Bass/Basso Cantante/Basso Cantabile

Lyric basses have the lightest bass quality, and their voices are agile and vibrant with a fast vibrato. They are found more often in Italian operas than in German works.

Their voices can easily be mistaken for baritones or bass-baritones because they can sing most of the baritone repertoire without problems. Their tessitura will still give them away as basses, though.

One of the best-known lyric basses from the beginning of the 20th century was Feodor Chaliapin. He virtually owned the title role in Mussorgsky's opera *Boris Godunov*.

Ezio Pinza and Samuel Ramey are also well-known in this category.

Lee Hazlewood and Hoyt Axton had great lyric bass voices on the lighter side.

### Dramatic Bass

Think a shade darker than the lyric basses but just as deep and powerful, and you have a dramatic bass. They have a very mature, powerful, and deep character to their voices.

One of the greatest dramatic basses in modern music was the late great Leonard Cohen.

We think of Hans Hotter, James Morris, and Friedrich Schorr in the opera.

### Basso Buffo

The basso buffo, meaning comic bass in Italian, is a subdivision of the dramatic bass. They specialize in Italian comic operas such as Rossini's *Barber of Seville* and Mozart's *Cosi fan Tutte*.

The roles demand excellent comic timing and the ability to sing words at a lightning-fast pace as generally blundering, foolish, lovable characters.

## Basso Profundo

The lowest human voice possible is the deep bass. The typical range is G1 or lower.

The record for the lowest voice in the world is held by a singer named Tim Storms. According to the Guinness record, he hit the G7 note that was measured at 0.189 Hz. In addition, Storms also holds the record for having the widest vocal range of all human beings: An astonishing 10 octaves!

Bassi profundi don't have fast vibratos; they rather have a solid quality to their voices that prefer to stay in the lower registers. Their vocal cords are thicker and longer than other voice types, and some basses struggle to attain a head voice at all.

Well-known operatic deep basses include Boris Christoff, René Pape, and Martti Talvela.

Unfortunately, they are not much "in fashion" at the moment in modern music. Some of the greats of yesteryear include Paul Robeson and Tennessee Ernie Ford.

Russian basses are in a subcategory of their own with the exceptionally deep, dark sound they can produce. They're also called oktavists. Remember Ivan Rebroff?

# EXPLORING YOUR VOCAL RANGE

A person's voice type and vocal range are not the same, but most people confuse these two terms, hampering their learning process. This chapter talks about vocal range, defining what it is and how to identify yours.

Mixing up voice type with vocal range is a common error that many novice singers make. For instance, when asked about their vocal range, they'd often reply by stating that they are a baritone or a soprano. Contrary to this misconception, voice range is not the same as voice type.

With some knowledge of music and consistent practice, you can easily identify your vocal range and develop your voice type to make the most of your singing career.

## THE DIFFERENCE BETWEEN VOICE TYPE AND VOCAL RANGE

While voice type is determined based on certain qualities, voice range refers to the full spectrum of notes that a singer's voice can touch, starting from the lowest note and reaching the uppermost note possible.

The term vocal range refers to every sound a person can utter, from low to high, and not only to notes that can be utilized for performing. A low grunt and a high screech all count as part of your vocal range.

Normally, an untrained singer would have limited vocal range compared to an experienced singer who has developed their range through practice and a better understanding of vocal techniques. Some voices can also be developed to a wider range than others, but everyone can expand their range.

In classical singing, the useful part of a singer's range is a defining factor. The consistency of their timbre and the range of pitches that the singer can carry over an orchestra without amplification are considered. It is sometimes called a professional singer's "publicly performable" range (O'Connor, 2020c).

This could mean, for example, that a mezzo-soprano could be classified as having a range of two octaves, although she might have access to another half an octave either way.

Choral music does not put the same emphasis on the useful range because there is a multitude of voices to carry the tune over the accompaniment.

Contemporary music always employs sound boosting equipment, so more of a modern-style singer's range becomes useful.

## WHAT IS YOUR REGISTER?

The register is another term that can confuse beginner singers. It does not consist of only one aspect of the voice.

The register comprises a series of sounds that are produced in the same vibratory pattern by the vocal folds, and they all have the same quality within a certain range of pitches.

A common distinction found among speech therapists is to divide the human voice into three registers: Chest, middle, and head. Some males have a very low, almost grunting register called vocal fry, while some females have what is known as a whistle register, which is very high.

The last two are mostly classified as chest and head registers extensions rather than registers in their own right.

Let's look at each of the registers in more detail.

## Vocal Fry Register

Some people call this low sound a pulse register or a glottal scrape/rattle. The sound quality is cracking, croaking, and rattling.

During sound production, the glottal opening is not closed completely, and the air is allowed to come through slowly. The vocal folds are slack, and a floppy, vibrating mass is formed.

Many contemporary voice teachers use this technique on their students as a type of relaxing exercise. However, prolonged or frequent use of vocal fry can damage the vocal cords, and caution should be exercised.

Vocal fry is often used at the beginning of phrases as a type of embellishment in contemporary styles, but it can lead to the loss of some notes in the higher register.

## Chest Register

Also known as the normal voice register, the chest register is, for the most part, equal to a speaking voice. Men talk exclusively in their chest registers, while women use both the chest and head registers.

The chest voice sounds darker and warmer than the middle and head voices. The vocal folds are thick and more involved in phonation than in other registers.

## Middle Register

For males, this register is also known as the *zona di passaggio*. That means it lies between the break from the chest voice to the middle register and the transition from the middle register to the head voice.

The octave that forms the middle register in females is also known as the medium voice.

The sound quality produced in this register is a mixture of the chest and head registers.

## Head Register

You know you're singing in your head register or head voice when you feel all the sound resonating in your sinuses and skull.

The vocal folds stretch to create higher notes, and the sound quality is lighter and crisper.

The head voice can be carried down into the chest register without damage to the voice, but the sound would be thin and without color.

## Falsetto

Although it is mainly associated with men, all singers have a falsetto voice. The sound quality is similar to a female voice. It is not a synonym or replacement for a full head voice, although it runs parallel to the head register in pitch.

Strictly speaking, falsetto is more of a tonal quality than a register. The vocal folds become extremely thin and stretched, and the pitch has to be regulated through breathing. The sound does not exhibit overtones.

Falsetto has its place, and it is not to be used as a substitute for the vocal control needed to produce a full head voice in higher passages of songs.

When females use their falsetto range, the sound is not much different from the head voice. Applying the same techniques as men do to achieve falsetto will most likely only result in a wobbly, breathy sound.

## Whistle Register

Also known as the flageolet register, it is the highest range the human voice is capable of. It is above the female head voice, but there is no discernible bridge from the head to the whistle register, which is why many people consider the whistle register to be merely an extension of the head voice that some women are capable of.

The sound quality is noticeably crisp and penetrating, just like a whistle.

Practicing the flageolet can benefit any higher voice type, even if it is not actively used in performances. It will make the high notes even more accessible by strengthening the vocal folds.

# A FEW IMPORTANT TERMS

Various terms are often mentioned when exploring your vocal type and range that can confuse novices. Understanding what they are about will make it easier to identify your range.

## Melody vs. Harmony

The melody is a linear progression of notes creating a cohesive tune. The harmony in the melody is a collection of notes happening simultaneously, as in a chord.

There is a clear distinction between the harmony and the melodic line of a song.

## Pitch

Your perception of a note, whether it is high or low or in-between, is the pitch. The pitch is determined by the frequency of the sound waves that reach your ears. The object making the sound vibrates, creating a pressure wave. The pressure wave triggers an electric signal in our brains that activates the auditory circuit.

When the frequency increases because the air is vibrating faster or decreases because the air is vibrating slower, we perceive it as a change in pitch. High notes have a high frequency, and low notes have a low frequency.

"Singing on pitch" refers to the ability to mentally align yourself with the frequency of the sound you're hearing and produce a sound on the same frequency.

Some individuals have what is known as "perfect pitch." That means they can align their sound to the frequency they hear and identify it without having any reference points in other notes around it. It is more than just singing in tune, and not everyone has the gift.

## Octave

An octave consists of eight full notes. The endpoint is eight notes higher than the starting point.

The top note of the octave will have twice the frequency of the bottom note, although their designations will be the same.

Playing the top and bottom notes together creates harmony pleasing to the human ear.

## Interval

An interval is a distance between two specific pitches. It can be any number of notes.

Some intervals create a harmonious effect for our perception, while others sound discordant.

# THE IMPORTANCE OF TONE

When you listen to two singers performing the same song in the same key, the recordings would not sound identical. You would be able to distinguish one voice from the other clearly.

The reason for that is tone. It can also be described as the color of the voice. It is individual and characteristic and should be developed to establish your specific sound as you progress in your vocal studies.

Some singers are lucky enough to have a beautiful tone from the start, but most of us have to work at it.

We have touched on formants in an earlier chapter, but their role is crucial in determining your distinctive tone. The voice of a young child or an untrained adult singer sometimes sounds simple and 'thin' because the formants, or overtones, have not been developed.

These resonant frequencies must stay constant through the different registers and should not be influenced by the pitch.

In a speech, only the two or three lowest formants are produced. In singing, however, there are five or six relevant formants. A trained singing voice exhibits equal strength in the lower and upper formants.

## The Role of Formants

Let's first recap what formants are about. The human voice does not consist of only one tone. There is a basic frequency known as the fundamental and five to six supplemental tones known as overtones or formants.

The formants are integer multiples of the fundamental frequency, and they are roughly 1,000Hz apart from each other.

Together, the fundamental and formant frequencies comprise the pitches that give color and character to humans' speaking and singing voices. A trained voice exhibits the ideal balance between the darker parts called the Oscuro elements, and the lighter side called the Chiaro elements.

Formants are resonant acoustic elements that have their origin in the shape and size of the vocal tract and its resonating chambers. Some overtones are emphasized above others, depending on the individual's vocal tract. Adult women, for instance, have a shorter vocal tract than men and their formant frequencies are 15 percent higher than those of men. The higher frequencies are emphasized in women, and the lower ones are much softer or even unheard. The opposite situation is true for adult men.

The timbre of any voice is strongly dependent on the pattern formed by the first three formants. Individuals can change their pattern within limits by moving the articulators or directing the sound through the nasal cavity instead of through the mouth.

Formant determines the quality of vowels, producing a voice's unique character. The two lowest ones largely make up a person's speaking voice, but in singing, the upper formants are the factors that make up the qualities we use to distinguish one voice from the other.

An interesting addition to the usual formants is what has become known as the singer's formant. That is found only in trained singing voices, and it allows singers to make themselves heard even above a large orchestra.

Swedish scientist Johan Sundberg studied recordings of the tenor Jussi Bjoerling in the 1970s and found a large hump of sound that occurred around 3,000Hz. The sound peak was especially noticeable when Bjoerling was performing with a large orchestra (National Center for Voice and Speech, 2021).

An orchestra produces a huge amount of sound energy around 500Hz, but then it steadily diminishes in the higher frequencies. A trained vocalist harnesses the energy in the upper formants of the voice and concentrates it at the point where the orchestra sound is weakening. This process does not occur consciously but results from years of practicing and performing. Professional singers achieve the singer's formant by lowering the larynx while lifting the blade of the tongue.

## Fine-Tuning the Formants

The good news here is that big, positive changes can come from making small changes. Changing the shape of the vocal tract from a perfectly round tube to something different will change the frequencies of the sounds produced and the frequencies that are emphasized or resonated in the vocal delivery.

Put in simpler terms, opening the jaw wider at the right time or changing the tongue's position will change both the shape of the vocal tract and the positioning of the formants, resulting in a change in the perceived voice.

Lifting the corners of the mouth increases all formant frequencies while opening the mouth cavity wider by lowering the jaw will strengthen the first formant frequency. The sound will sound brighter and livelier.

Even on vowels such as 'iii,' a darker sound will result from protruding the lips and lowering the larynx because the tongue will be in a lowered position instead of the normal forward position.

Adjusting formant frequencies by these vocal tract manipulations is known as formant tuning. Through his research, Sundberg identified the locations of the formant frequencies in the vocal tract.

- What we commonly call the depth of a singer's voice relates to the first formant. The shape of the oral cavity and pharynx, which are in turn influenced by how wide the jaw is opened, particularly determines the sound of the first formant.
- The second formant is sensitive to the position and form of the tongue. This formant is related to the formation of vowels.
- The tip of the tongue and the size of the opening between the tongue and the lower teeth determine the quality of the third formant.
- The fourth and fifth formants are not easy to control by adjusting the vocal tract.

It is important to understand that changes in the pitch of a voice do not alter the formants. Only changes to the shape of the vocal tract have that effect.

Ponder the significance of this statement for a moment. It means to you, as a singer, that singing a high or low note in itself does not create the problems you might perceive in the quality of your singing and the sound of your voice. The changes you make to your vocal tract while singing, even if you don't realize you're making them, are the causes of your sound problems.

## Overtone Singing: Formants in Action

An excellent example of overtones in practice is overtone singing. Although the term overtone singing is used interchangeably with throat singing, it is somewhat of a misnomer. Real throat singing as practiced in some cultures, such as the Xhosa nation in South Africa, and some groups in Papua-New Guinea do not involve overtones.

We generally understand formant or overtone singing allows one voice to use all the overtones present to produce different sounds in different pitches. It originated in Mongolia and was used in the chants of Tibetan monks for centuries. The rest of the world only learned about the practice when the monks were forced to flee their country for the safety of India when the People's Republic of China invaded Tibet in 1950.

Someone who mastered the technique to an amazing extent is Nestor Kornblum, the co-director and co-founder of the International Association of Sound Therapy (Harmonic Sounds, 2021).

Listen to his rendition of the song "Amazing Grace," using his voice only for an outstanding illustration of overtone singing. There are no instruments involved! You will find the free video on Youtube at **https://www.youtube.com/watch?v=nPu9XMMY1Y8** (Harmonic Voices, 2013).

# VIBRATO

Another often misunderstood component of tone is a singer's vibrato. It is perceived as a desirable quality giving warmth and character to the voice. Vibrato can be fast or slow and wide or narrow.

The vibrato mechanism is that a rapid varying of pitch occurs in succession. The pitches are very close together and should not stray further than a semitone from the note of the melody.

Listeners only hear the average between the pitch differences and interpret it as one sound.

Voice researchers are not quite sure why vibrato happens. Still, they agree that the body's need for muscle relaxation during sustained and intense activity, such as high notes, could be possible (O'Connor, 2020f).

The larynx muscles develop an alternating pulse to maintain their equilibrium and protect the vocal folds. The muscles experience constant pressure from the air and its movement through the glottis, and it tires them. It is the same principle as when your arm muscles start to shake when you're holding something heavy for a long period.

The tongue, epiglottis (the flap of skin covering the top of the larynx), and the pharyngeal wall also vibrate with the laryngeal muscles. This sympathetic movement is sometimes visible on the outside of the neck and is no reason for alarm.

The basic position of the larynx should remain stable. Otherwise, the voice will exhibit a tremolo or wobble. A tremolo is a rapid, narrow vibrato, while a wobble is a wide, slow vibrato that sounds if it occurs on only one pitch.

Besides the natural vibrato in the voice, artificial vibrato can also be learned and used for effect in certain passages.

Artificial vibrato has to be used sparingly and only if your breathing technique is solid enough not to be thrown off course by it. Using a pronounced, wide vibrato at the end of every sustained note becomes just as boring as not using vibrato at all.

It is necessary to understand that having the skill to produce an exaggerated vibrato on demand does not make anyone a better singer. It can, in fact, be unhealthy for an untrained singer. When fake pulses are produced, the pressure created in the larynx will establish bad singing habits like a tensed jaw and tongue and hold the singer's overall development back. A classic example of induced vibrato is Whitney Houston's performance in the movie *The Body Guard*. She produced the vibrating sound by quivering her jaw and moving her tongue rapidly instead of using her natural voice. That adds unnecessary complications to singing and can make a novice feel like they will never master good singing.

If your voice coach is telling you right at the outset to learn vibrato by quivering your jaw or rapidly sucking in and releasing your abdomen, you should see some red lights flickering.

A voice that is allowed to develop without forcing anything produces a beautiful natural vibrato over time, and the voice will be enhanced without any harm having been done. Vibrato is not something to be added. It can be suppressed or allowed at will when it is part of the voice but forcing an artificial sound is never a good idea.

## Developing Normal Vibrato

A steady and controlled airflow, solid muscle support, and coordinated movement along the whole vocal tract are essential for a consistent natural vibrato to develop. The ideal vibrato rate is about six to eight oscillations per second.

Uneven breath pressure will result in the vocal folds separating and vibrating at different tempos, making the vibrato unstable and unattractive.

Vibrato development, therefore, goes hand-in-hand with time, patience, and practice. Good vocal technique will produce a clear, bright, and resonant voice ready to employ vibrato.

The good technique also leads to a more relaxed vocal delivery, and a relaxed voice can allow the mechanism by which vibrato works. A tense singer will not have any vibrato, even if it is present under normal circumstances. The tension also extends to the laryngeal muscles, and they can't perform their relaxing pulsations, resulting in extreme vocal fatigue.

## Is Vibrato Essential?

Proponents of induced vibrato will have you believe that a 'straight sounding voice is not attractive and will never be popular because it is inferior. That simply is not true.

Suppose your natural inclination is a voice with little or no vibrato. In that case, your tone and color will be enough to establish you as a good singer—provided your technique is solid.

A straight voice can be vibrant and resonant, as in the case of the immensely popular 1970s artist Karen Carpenter. Her voice was so special and emotive that vibrato would have detracted from her impact on listeners.

Choral singers are also discouraged from singing with vibrato. Several singers all vibrating their voices at different rates could make the choir sound off-pitch. The exception to this rule is an opera chorus that often comprises several soloists in their own right.

# FINDING YOUR OWN VOCAL RANGE

Most of us in the singing world do not possess a range of nearly four octaves like Michael Jackson had, but finding your range and exploring it fully is essential to your singing success.

The most common size for a vocal range is between two and two-and-a-half octaves.

## Warm-Up!

It is always important to warm up your vocal cords before doing any singing, but it is even more crucial when exploring the limits of your voice.

Hum a couple of tunes or sing a moderate scale up and down a few times. Do your warmup exercises on different vowel sounds to get your lips, tongue, etc., loosened too.

## Start Low

Using a piano, keyboard, or piano app with a simulated keyboard, identify the lowest note you can sing with ease in your normal voice and hold for three seconds without wavering. The sound should not crack at all and have the same sound quality as the notes, just higher—it should not sound growling or more breathy, for instance.

Choose an open vowel sound like 'ooh' or 'ahh' and start a couple of notes higher than where you think your lowest note is. Go down the scale gradually until you reach your limit.

Remember, the note has to be sustainable to count.

## Find Your Highest Note

Repeat the process to find your highest note, working up this time. The final note should not put any strain on your voice or throat and be on the pitch without screeching.

Men should not go into falsetto for this exercise. If you do, see if you can change the falsetto note into an open head voice quality. If not, the note you reached in falsetto mode will only count as a possible secondary highest.

## Identifying Your Range

The notation used to identify pitches and registers follows the International Standards Organization (ISO) system to designate registers to determine any range.

It always starts from middle C, which is designated as C4. The C one octave above that will be C5, the F two octaves below that will be F2, and so on.

The usual ranges by voice type are:

- Soprano: C4 to C6.
- Mezzo Soprano: A3 to A5.
- Contralto: F3 to F5.
- Tenor: C3 to C5.
- Baritone: G2 to G4.
- Bass: E2 to E5.

These ranges only show the most common and approximate values. Individual voices in the same category can sometimes sing lower or higher, depending on their specific vocal traits.

# IMPROVING YOUR VOCAL RANGE

Now that you have identified your current workable range, it is time to expand it through training and practice.

Always put the health of your vocal organs above expansion. It is natural to be impatient for growth, but do not push your voice too quickly and aggressively past the limits that you can feel in a certain exercise. Allow your range to develop gradually. You will reap the benefits in the long run if you take it slower in the beginning.

## Tips for Vocal Health

- Try making it a habit not to talk too loudly or high-pitched at noisy events such as parties.
- Don't overdo the karaoke if you have a coaching session or performance coming up.
- Sleep seven to nine hours every night. Physical stamina is essential in vocal health and endurance.
- Hydrate, but not with cold beverages right before singing. That will cause your vocal folds to shrink and vibrate slower, reducing the quality of your voice.
- In some people, dairy products add copious mucous to the throat. Don't wait until the night of the performance to find out if you're one of them.
- Stay away from food and drinks that can dry out your throat and mouth. Citrus, alcohol, and coffee should only be used in moderation.
- Allergy medications such as OTC antihistamine tablets or flu remedies are notorious for drying all mucous membranes, including the throat and vocal folds. Cough drops and liquids containing menthol will have the same drying effect.
- Overly spicy, sour, or astringent foods and liquids can irritate the throat.

- Sanitize your hands regularly to avoid colds. If you get sick, treat the infection right away before it can escalate into something dramatic.
- Treat a sore throat with warm decaffeinated tea with a drop of fresh lemon juice and a small slice of fresh ginger added. Speak as little as possible. Gargling with a saline solution will also help.
- Use a humidifier at home, especially at night, if you live in a dry climate.
- Rinse your sinuses with a saline solution using a neti pot if you suffer from sinus congestion.

## Start Small

Even Olympic athletes can't shave off a minute from their time in a month, so why would you want to force yourself to add a whole octave in a short time?

Gentle and consistent are your keywords here. Set yourself attainable goals that won't strain your voice, and keep practicing consistently.

Try to expand in increments of one half-note at the bottom or top at a time. Work until you have that half note securely in your useful range before moving on. No one can tell you how long that will or should take because your voice is as unique as you are.

## Pay Extra Attention to Warming Up

You will be testing and challenging the current outer limits of your voice during exercises to expand your range. Your warm-up routine should be even more gradual than usual.

Start by humming some scales, ascending half-a-step every time. When you get to the top note with which you are comfortable at that time, reverse the process and move down the scale as far as you can.

Don't progress to singing vowels before your vocal cords start feeling a bit loose and the sound comes easier.

## Expansion Exercises

- The siren exercise discussed earlier is excellent to use on a warmed-up voice. You can take the slide as low and as high as you can go.
- A lip trill is a safe but powerful exercise. Sing the sound 'uhh' on a comfortable pitch and allow your lips to flap together from the air you are expelling. This puts your vocal folds into a relaxed position, making it easier for them to vibrate. Gradually take your pitch up (or down, depending on your direction of expansion).
- Sing your scales on an 'ng' sound as in the word 'rung.' This sound keeps your tongue in a completely relaxed position and allows your vocal folds maximum vibration room. Try to sing through one-and-a-half octave up and down for this exercise.
- Do the same now with an open sound like 'gee' as in the word 'geese.'
- Bring your inner brat out to play and sing on a bright 'nay' sound as a toddler on a playground would do. That's an even wider sound than the previous one, and you might find you go higher or lower without even thinking about it.
- End your expansion session by singing the word 'mum' through all your scales.

Expanding your range is the first step on the road toward a beautiful performance so that you can tell your story to your audience in the best way possible.

# THE PERFECT SINGING POSTURE

Singing is not just about controlling your voice but also about how well you conduct your body postures. This chapter discusses the fundamentals of keeping a good posture for maximizing your singing and enjoying it to the fullest.

Many new singers wrongly believe that singing starts and ends with controlling the voice and breath. While these are integral elements of mastering the art, they aren't the only ones.

Keeping the right body and facial posture is critical to improving singing. Improper posture can sink the most talented singer.

The good news is that you don't have to eat the elephant all at once; with proper techniques and regular practice, you can improve your posture and improve your singing.

## WHY IS POSTURE IMPORTANT?

Your body is just as much your instrument as your voice is. It is an instrument that has to be flexible and well-conditioned.

The aim is to produce optimal sound without expending extra effort.

FIND YOUR OWN SINGING VOICE   #   69

To test this, you can sing a few phrases while holding the correct posture and then sing the same phrases in your original slouched position. You'll be amazed at the difference!

## Lengthening the Body

To maximize your body for breathing and resonating, it is necessary to stand up straight.

You can practice this any time you think about it, so it will be second nature to you when you get to singing. With the myriad of things to concentrate on when singing properly, you can cross posture off the list if you're already doing it automatically.

Imagine your spine is being pulled up toward the sky. Point your crown upward and your tailbone downward. This alignment will cause a slight forward shifting of the pelvis.

To help you get used to the proper alignment, you can start by standing with your back against a wall. Your head, shoulders, back, and heels all have to touch the wall.

Your chin should stay parallel to the ground. If you lift your chin too high, it will stretch your throat and vocal cords. Tucking in your chin will obstruct your airflow. Your jaw should be in a neutral position and your tongue down and relaxed.

Relax enough in this stance to remove any strain you might feel on any muscles. Keep your knees unlocked. That will allow your diaphragm to expand to the fullest.

If you can't get rid of your muscular tension, try shaking all over like a wet dog before assuming the right stance again.

Try a progressive muscle relaxation exercise once or twice a day and just before you drift off to sleep to cope with chronic tension.

- Sit or lie down comfortably in a place where you won't be disturbed for 15 to 20 minutes.
- Close your eyes, empty your mind of all thoughts, and become aware of the sounds you hear around you. Don't think about the

sounds or try to identify them. Hear them and let them go like fish darting through a pond.

- Starting with your toes and feet, let them go limp and loose. Feel the lightness this brings.
- Allow the loose lightness to move to your ankles and calves. Enjoy the feeling of freedom from tension.
- Move the relaxation progressively up your body, through your upper legs and thighs, hips, pelvis, abdomen, ribs, arms, shoulders, hands, throat, neck, and face.
- Feel your whole body drifting lightly and freely and enjoy the loose, relaxed feeling.
- Open your eyes when you feel ready and carry on with your day (or slip into sleep), taking the free and relaxed sensation with you.

## Maximize Your Breath

Relaxed shoulders that are held down and slightly backward will open up your airways. Rotate your shoulders a couple of times forward and backward before starting your vocal exercises to get them loose.

While holding your body in the proper lengthened position, concentrate on feeling that your rib cage is lifted and open. Don't puff out your chest in any way. To help you achieve the right feeling, put your arms behind your back and try to touch your elbows.

Incorporating everything said about breathing in a previous chapter, put your hand on your upper abdomen while you breathe to make sure your diaphragm is engaged.

Once you're comfortable in a regular breathing rhythm, let your arms hang loosely and relaxedly by your side. Hold your hands slightly away from your body and relax your fingers and hands.

## Create a Solid Foundation

Feeling securely anchored and balanced will help you relax your body to concentrate on your vocal delivery.

Don't lock your knees and rather bend them slightly to help keep your legs loose. Locked knees and rigid legs cause tension in the upper body and interfere with blood circulation. That interference, combined with nervousness when performing, can bring about dizzy spells and a feeling of lightheadedness.

Your feet should be the same width as your shoulders apart and flat on the ground. If you keep them too close together, it might become difficult to stay balanced. Putting them wide apart will expend unnecessary energy to keep the stance. If needed, put one foot slightly in front of the other to keep your balance.

Keep more weight on the balls of your feet than on your heels to help prevent your knees from locking.

# FACIAL POSTURE

The correct posture for your face is just as important as your body because you use your face muscles extensively to produce a good sound.

You also need to use your facial expressions effectively to convey the message of your music to your audience.

Understanding the anatomy of the mouth can help you make a clearer, brighter sound, avoid straining your vocal cords, and improve the overall quality of your voice.

## The Tongue

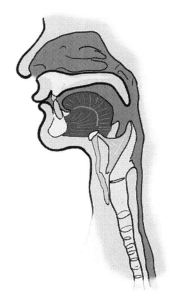

A cross-section showing how the tongue is anchored to the voice box.

The tongue plays an important role in a singer's life because it can significantly change the sound and placement of a note, either for better or worse.

There are eight muscles in the tongue, making it an agile organ that can help focus your sound.

Too much tension in the tongue will interfere with the vocal quality and positioning of the sounds. Try to move your tongue from side to side in your mouth without moving your jaw. If you struggle to do that, your tongue is too tense.

When a singer is not actively engaged in forming words, the correct tongue placement is the same as yawning. Practice that feeling a few times before you start your warmup routine.

The tongue plays such a big role because the tongue muscles go back into the throat and are joined to the voice box. Holding it in a pulled-up position will constrict the throat, hindering breathing and muffling the sound.

This is especially important when singing high notes. The mouth has to be opened wide to allow maximum resonance and air movement, and if the tongue is in the way, it becomes difficult to sing on pitch and with volume.

## The Teeth and Jaw

Have you ever seen a baby crying with clenched teeth? Impossible, right? The same principle applies to singing. If you want to produce a big, unforced sound, you must relax your jaw and open your mouth.

When the mouth is not open wide enough, the vocal cords will strain in an attempt to generate more volume and reach the required pitch. That can lead to permanent damage.

If your tongue is tense, there is a good chance that your jaw will experience the same. It is a good idea to massage all your face muscles before starting your vocal exercises. That will help them get ready to open up and move as they should.

A good way of learning what the right open sensation in your mouth and throat feels like is to pretend you're yawning without opening your lips as you would in a boring conversation when you don't want the host to see you yawning.

Here are a few more quick and effective ways to loosen your jaw muscles:

- Open your mouth slightly, move your lower jaw to the right, hold it for a second or two, and return to the center position. Then do the same to the left.
- Repeat the first exercise, holding your finger on one side of your jaw while moving the lower jaw. The movement should be smooth, not jerky and uneven.
- Open your mouth again slightly and move your lower jaw forward. Feel the stretch under your chin for a second or two before moving your jaw back and relaxing.

## The Soft Palate

The soft palate separates the nasal cavity and nasal section of the pharynx from the mouth and jaw. It is flexible and moves as the air coming from the vocal folds touches it.

Lifting the soft palate increases the sound cavity and improves resonance. This action happens automatically, and it is unnecessary to stress about it or try to lift the soft palate mechanically. Interfering with this movement in isolation will increase tension in the mouth and throat instead of decreasing it.

If you want to know what a soft palate in the right position feels like, you should laugh. Become aware of the slight stretching sensation in the back of your mouth—that is, your raised soft palate.

Even when you only smile, the soft palate lifts and creates a room that increases vocal control. There is something to be said for singing with a smile!

## Mouth Shaping

Choose your mouth opening according to the pitch
you're singing at and the vowel you are forming.

The opening of the mouth and positioning of the articulators are known as the embouchure. It comes from the French word *bouche*, which means 'mouth.'

There are two types of embouchures, vertical and horizontal. Each has its own uses.

When the mouth is opened vertically, it is great for open vowels, high notes, and creating a more brittle, metallic edge to the voice. There should not be any excessive jaw movement in vertical embouchure because that will destabilize the sound quality and vibrato.

The horizontal embouchure feels slightly less natural, but it reduces excessive jaw movement. Open vowels like 'eee' and 'oohh' are brighter and easier to form in this mouth position.

# THE THROAT

The most conflicting opinions and techniques in the study of vocal arts can be found on this topic. Everyone agrees that an open throat is essential to creating the biggest possible air and sound space. However, some of the ways advocated attaining this vary widely, from useless to potentially damaging.

It is important to be aware of the misconceptions about the throat and the mechanisms involved because adopting the wrong technique will lead to frustration and a disappointing sound, at best. At worst, you might end up with so much tension in your face, jaw, and neck that the pain will stop your singing, as well as damage to the vocal folds.

All the points previously discussed in this chapter come together when we look at the singer's throat. The soft palate, larynx, articulators, facial muscles, and mouth shape have to work together to produce a healthy, free, and bright sound. The sense of release to be experienced in the throat is intended to remove all feelings of a throttled or stifled sound.

Some teachers tell their students to keep feeling as if they're yawning, even after taking the initial breath on that sensation. Others use imagery by advising their students to "drink in the breath," forcing the throat open.

## What Not To Do

It is important not to confuse an open mouth with an open throat. Opening the mouth too wide, instead of just dropping the jaw enough to produce a clear sound, will increase tension in the larynx, lower the soft palate, and hinder effective closure of the vocal folds—exactly the opposite of what you want to achieve.

The tongue will get pushed down toward the larynx, creating an added obstruction to airflow and sound production. Think back to the last time you tried to keep talking while stifling a yawn. What did your voice sound like?

The same condition is also likely to occur when the student is told to feel like they're swallowing an egg or something big—the larynx will get depressed by the tongue, and a throaty, hollow sound will emerge.

Concentrating on the sensation of yawning during singing also produces a hollow tone that sounds unnatural and is not pleasing to listen to. In this position, the tongue tends to flatten, and the articulators cannot do their job properly.

Another senseless piece of advice some vocal teachers are fond of is instructing their students to look surprised while singing. Besides looking ridiculous during a performance, the sound will be of poor quality because of all the tension a facial posture with raised eyebrows, a creased forehead, and flared nostrils create.

Any facial expressions that are encouraged during coaching should be aimed at helping the students communicate the message of their music.

The surprised look is not to be confused with the lifting of the zygomatic muscles, which will be discussed in the next section.

## Techniques That Do Work

Lifting the zygomatic muscles deliberately, conditioned adds space in the sound cavity without increasing tension in the face, jaw, and neck muscles.

It involves assuming a pleasant, relaxed facial expression without actually smiling by lifting the cheeks using the zygomatic muscles. These muscles lift the corners of the mouth when smiling.

We are not used to keeping the zygomatics engaged for an extended period, and they have to be conditioned and strengthened through repeated exercise. In the beginning, you might feel them twitching and quivering after a few minutes.

Another useful technique is to inhale a soft 'k' sound. That aids the natural lifting of the soft palate and lowers the larynx when we inhale. It also ensures the tongue is separated from the soft palate and in a healthy singing position.

This is a natural and anatomically sound way to achieve an open throat. There is no dramatic effort involved, and the pleasant facial expression will go a long way to reach your audience.

In the initial stages of this facial posture, before it has become second nature to you, breaks in your technique are likely to occur when you switch between registers. Pay particular attention to the change from the middle to the head registers.

You can condition your larynx and pharynx to adopt this posture by forming the neutral sound 'uh' or the open 'aah' before morphing it into the vowel you will be using for your vocal exercise. That establishes the pharynx (the back of the throat) in the correct, open position, and it is easier to remain aware of the right feeling while singing the other sounds.

This strategy encourages a natural sense of "getting everything to work together." It will remove students' sense of being overwhelmed and the tendency to stress about all the new things that must be mastered. They understand that they just have to allow their automatic anatomical processes to function properly. It will also remove the temptation to go for a quick fix because the vocal coaching sessions seem impossibly complicated.

It is dangerous to tell someone to open the throat and lower the larynx without explaining how it works because that will cause them to try to achieve it in any way possible, leading to tension and bad-sounding voices. Unhealthy habits form stealthily, and before you know it, you might have nodules on your vocal folds and serious throat problems.

# SCANNING THE DYNAMICS OF A SONG

Analyzing a song will help you delve deeper into its dynamics, thereby improving your approach toward interpreting and singing it. Studying the dynamics will show you what makes the song great and guide you through adding your magic to make it even better.

This chapter will explore certain techniques for analyzing songs. It is imperative to take a good look at each song you consider performing to break down and understand its dynamics.

## TOP TIPS FOR ANALYZING MUSIC

Analyzing a song typically starts with understanding the lyrics, knowing the harmonic and chord structure, and learning the melodies used. It will make it easier to decide if a specific song is suitable to your voice and style and whether you will be able to put real passion into performing it.

The analysis can be done in various ways, but we'll discuss the top ways to get the job done quickly and efficiently.

## Draw Up a Structural Map

Firstly, identify the parts of the song. That could include an intro, verses, refrain, bridge, more verses, and the outro or ending.

Draw a straight line on a big enough piece of paper and write the timestamps where all the elements occur on the line. The intro would start at 0'00", the first verse could start at 0'48", the refrain at 2'50", etc.

It does not matter if you're not sure what to call a section, just identify it as an element.

Think about the dynamics your map is showing you. For Instance, are there lengthy instrumental sections that can slow the song down and lose its momentum? Are there many more repeats of the refrain than would seem balanced when you look at the number of verses? How will you make all those repeats interesting to keep the song alive?

## Identify the Instrumental Riffs and Hooks

A riff is a short, recurring melody that features throughout the song. A hook is a part of the song that stands out. Hooks are not repeated as often as riffs and, for that reason, make a greater impact when they occur.

Decide in your mind whether the riffs are needed and the hooks are effective for interpreting the song.

In the classic 1965 Rolling Stones song "Satisfaction," the riff is used to start the song, and then it only appears again in the refrain.

A classic example of a hook can be heard in Neil Diamond's 1969 hit "Sweet Caroline." The chorus, in which the song's title is repeated, is so catchy that it's difficult to forget the tune once you've heard it.

## Take Note of the Chord Progressions

A chord or harmonic progression is a succession of chords that make up the development of the harmony in the song. The chords are played in a specific pattern that affects the song's sound.

Chords in major keys are perceived as bright and uplifting, while minor chords sound depressing or melancholy to us.

Compare the story of the song with the chord progression used. Does the pattern of progression strengthen the story or work against it? If there is a contrast, is it functional, or does it detract from the song? If the contrast is deliberate, will you be able to interpret and relate that message to your audience in such a way that the composer's intent will come through?

## Write Out the Lyrics

The lyrics form an extremely important part of a song. The audience has to be able to identify with the lyrics and appreciate their message. Otherwise, the song will fall flat.

Do you believe the song's message, and will you be able to identify with it, first of all, before you offer the story to someone else? Do the lyrics make sense to you?

Which parts of the lyrics carry the most emotion? Which parts should be emphasized?

Do the lyrics and the melody work together or against each other?

## Identify the Melody Parts

A song seldom consists of one simple melody. It is usually made up of melodic parts that are repeated and mixed throughout the song.

Take note of any repetitions. Are they functional?

Identify the highest and lowest notes and ensure they are within your comfortable range.

# TAKING CARE OF YOUR VOICE

Your voice is your most precious treasure as a singer. A singer not only has to improve their singing skills, but they also have to take care of the health of their voice. Your voice is the one element that will make or break your performance. The sooner you get into a habit of looking after your vocal health, the better it will work out for you.

It is imperative to preserve your voice and keep it in top condition. This chapter will discuss some techniques to keep a check on your voice. You will have heard some of the points about vocal health before, but they are so important that they should be repeated often.

Your general physical health should also get a workout if you want to ensure you stay on top of your singing game, and we'll cover that, too.

## YOUR VOCAL CORDS

Your vocal cords must be flexible, free from inflammation, smooth, and soft for the best performance. They are vulnerable to damage and should be protected.

## Warming Up

Warming up before singing is not negotiable, even if you do just the minimum. We have covered warming up routines extensively in an earlier chapter. Just a reminder: It should take you between 10 and 20 minutes, and don't forget about your facial muscles—they need loosening too.

Add another layer of protection by cooling down after your lesson, performance, or audition. Allow your voice to settle back into the normal speech range by doing gentle glides and sighs going down. Move your facial muscles to release any tension that might have built up there. Drop your jaw, stick out your tongue as far as it will go, and yawn a couple of times widely to lift your soft palate.

Cooling down need not take longer than five to 10 minutes.

## Hydration

Drinking water is a singer's best way to stay hydrated.

Dried-out vocal cords can only be hydrated from within because nothing that enters through the mouth touches the vocal folds. The esophagus is separate from the larynx to protect us from choking.

Be sure to drink enough pure water at room temperature throughout the day. Herbal tea that is not too hot is a good secondary hydrating measure.

Dried-out vocal cords will become irritated when used due to their lack of flexibility. That can lead to inflammation and serious damage.

Avoid drinking too much water right before singing, though. A waterlogged stomach will make diaphragm control and correct breathing difficult.

## Create a Humid Environment

The air you breathe can make a huge difference to the level of hydration in your vocal folds. If you live in a generally dry area or have to prepare for a concert during a dry season, running a humidifier in your home will help keep your instrument in top condition.

Dry air also makes breathing difficult and can cause respiratory infections.

## Take Regular "Vocal Naps"

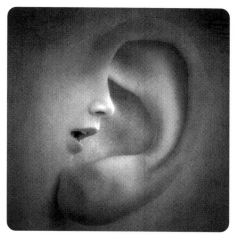

Whispering puts much strain on the voice.

It is recommended that you rest your voice for 10 minutes after every 60 minutes of singing. Rest implies no singing, talking, or whispering whatsoever.

Whispering requires significant effort to make yourself heard, which puts a huge amount of strain on your vocal cords. When you whisper, you talk without vibrating the vocal folds. They are stretched tight but are not allowed to vibrate, which can dry them out and fatigue them.

When you are in a cycle of preparation for a performance or other big event, you should stay as quiet as possible in the evenings and between rehearsals to give your voice some rest.

## Vocal Cord Disorders

This section is not intended to scare you silly but rather to make you aware of how serious damage to your voice can get if you don't take care of it. Your vocal gift is precious!

According to the experts at Johns Hopkins Medicine in Maryland, vocal disorders are mostly caused by abuse and misuse (Kaur Dhillon, 2021).

Some of the first symptoms you may notice include hoarseness for longer than two weeks in the absence of a cold or sinus infection, a sudden inability to reach the top notes in your register, breathy and raspy quality to the voice that was not introduced deliberately, and trouble swallowing or coughing.

In many cases, rest and hydration are all that's needed. If the problem is serious enough to require microsurgery, it is usually done in a day clinic. Patients rarely complain of severe pain afterward, only minor discomfort and a sore throat.

Complete voice rest is essential after any surgery. After two or three weeks, your doctor will give the go-ahead for you to start with voice therapy. This is to help with your recovery and teach you better habits to prevent a recurrence of the problem.

Depending on the seriousness of the disorder, you could also benefit from a session or two of psychotherapy to work through the emotional side of losing your voice, whether it is temporary or, hopefully not, permanent.

## Laryngitis

This condition is caused by inflammation of the vocal cords. A viral infection commonly causes inflammation, but overuse of the voice and exposure to harmful substances such as tobacco and excessive alcohol can bring it on too.

Early warning signs of laryngitis include a tickling or raw feeling in the throat, dryness, a weak, raspy voice, and a dry cough.

The inflammation causes the vocal folds to swell. That blocks the airflow through the folds, and the voice becomes hoarse or disappears altogether.

Acute laryngitis usually dissolves on its own if the voice is rested, enough fluids are taken in, and appropriate medication is taken to clear the symptoms of the viral infection. It can become chronic if the underlying cause is not taken care of.

Continued, forced use of the voice during a bout of laryngitis can damage the vocal cords irreparably and should be avoided at all costs.

## Nodules

Nodules are noncancerous bumps that form on the vocal folds, often in spots that experience the most pressure when the folds come together. They are similar to calluses.

Symptoms include an involuntary raspy, breathy quality to the voice, feeling there's something stuck in your throat, and a voice that suddenly "cuts out" while in use. It can also cause pain that shoots from ear to ear.

Nodules can vary in size from a pinhead to a pea. They interfere with the flow of air through the vocal folds, which changes the voice's pitch, strength, and color.

If hoarseness lasts for more than two weeks, it is advisable to see a doctor for confirmation. The possibility of something more serious underlying the nodules also has to be ruled out before treatment begins. Conditions such as acid reflux, allergies, sinusitis, and thyroid issues can all bring on the growth of nodules.

The first thing you will be prescribed is to rest your voice, combined with a few sessions with a speech therapist. The therapist can teach you how to use your voice safely and break any bad talking or singing habits you might have developed over the years.

If the nodules are very large or don't go away with treatment and rest, you might need to remove them surgically.

There is always a risk that the surgery might not be successful, as veteran British soprano Dame Julie Andrews discovered in 1997. She was left with enough scarring on her vocal folds that her four-octave soprano voice turned into a shaky alto with one octave, at best (Kettler, 2020). It is far better not to let nodules develop in the first place.

Many well-known singers have struggled with the issue and had to undergo surgery at some point in their careers. Mariah Carey, Miley Cyrus, Sir Elton John, Whitney Houston, Justin Timberlake, Natalie Dessay, and Luciano Pavarotti are a few of the famous performers who had to battle problems with their vocal cords.

The forming of nodules is very common in classical singers, but they seem reluctant to admit they ran into vocal injuries (Edwards, 2015). Although proper technique will go a long way to safeguard your vocal folds against them, all your good work can become undone by other unhealthy habits discussed later in this chapter.

Get medical help before it is too late to rescue your voice, and don't let any possible criticism of your technique hold you back.

## Polyps

Polyps are also noncancerous growths, just like nodules, but soft like blisters. The polyp can start off being filled with blood. The blood will resolve gradually, and a clear blister will remain.

The symptoms and effect on the voice are the same as with nodules. Their biggest difference with nodules is that they usually develop on only one side of the vocal cords, while nodules are commonly found in pairs, one on each side. They occur in varying shapes and sizes.

Besides the same treatment as for nodules, it is also helpful to avoid as much as possible clearing your throat harshly or coughing.

Most people don't need more than rest and plenty of fluids for the polyps to retreat on their own, given enough time—on average, about eight months.

Adele, the pop singer with the incredibly powerful, beautiful voice, learned this lesson the hard way. In 2011, she had to undergo surgery to repair polyps and cysts on her vocal cords. The operation seemed to be a great success, and three months later, Adele swept up six Grammys.

Six years later, still singing the way she used to, she pushed through with performances despite lesions developing again. The lesions burst during her singing, and she was left with permanent scars on her vocal folds. She had to disappear from the stage for a considerable time to regain her voice. Her relatively young age counted in her favor.

The tragic tale can be compared to a professional football player who gets ligament surgery and resumes playing too soon, pushing himself until he ends up having to quit playing for good.

The opera stars Rolando Villazón, Roberto Alagna, and Aleksandrs Antonenko had to walk off the stage midway through their performances because their abused voices just could not go on. Steroid injections before a performance can only go so far as to sustain vocal integrity.

## Cysts

Vocal cysts are firm mounds of tissue surrounded by a fluid-filled sac or membrane. They are less common than nodules and polyps.

The symptoms, effects, and treatments are the same as the other two types of lesions.

### Vocal Cord Paralysis

One of the more serious vocal disorders is paralysis. It will cause the voice to sound weak, and the person will experience frequent choking while eating because the folds (one or both) can't close properly.

The condition results when the nerve signals to the larynx are disrupted. Viral infections such as Lyme disease, the Epstein-Barr virus, herpes, surgery going wrong, injuries to the throat, neck, or chest, stroke, some neurological disorders such as Parkinson's disease, and certain types of cancer can bring it on.

A sudden loss of pitch, an increased need to take breaths even when speaking, noisy breath, losing the gag reflex, and a marked loss of volume in both speech and singing are symptoms to look out for.

Surgery is usually required, although the problem reverses itself in some people.

### Cancer

The vocal folds, larynx, and pharynx can develop cancer.

The main causes are prolonged irritation by tobacco and alcohol, untreated GERD and acid reflux, exposure to certain viral infections, and a diet deficient in fruits and vegetables.

Hoarseness is the main symptom of cancer of the vocal folds, and a biopsy will confirm the preliminary diagnosis. It has a good prognosis for successful treatment if caught early enough.

The main symptoms of laryngeal cancer are a sore throat, hoarseness, trouble swallowing, and ear pain.

Your doctor will physically examine your neck and throat for any lumps or other abnormal growths and take a biopsy of the laryngeal lining. A CT-scan or magnetic resonance imaging (MRI) may also be done.

The prognosis depends on the patient's age, the development stage of cancer, and the location of the tumor.

Pharyngeal cancer is commonly called throat cancer, and it includes the whole region inside the neck that starts at the nose and ends at the top of the trachea and esophagus. The base of the tongue and the soft palate are also included.

The first symptom patients usually spot is a painless lump in the upper part of the neck. Persistent headaches, a chronically blocked nose, nosebleeds, facial pain, and hearing issues such as tinnitus can also occur.

# THE THROAT

A healthy throat as a whole is essential for good vocal quality. Straining and pushing from the throat while singing is a big no-no. Your throat should always be as relaxed as possible while your diaphragm and breath do the work.

Pay attention if your throat hurts; don't just ignore the pain and try to push through it. Try to identify the cause, type, and location before grabbing the lozenges or cough mixture and carrying on with singing.

When it is more of a burning sensation high in the throat, where the nasal cavity and the throat meet, it is possibly due to a respiratory infection. Singing very softly and for a limited time can be done safely if it is essential to practice a piece that can't wait. Hydrate yourself even better than usual and stay aware of any changes—if the burning intensifies or changes into a persistent ache, stop immediately.

If you experience a dull pain lower in your throat rather than the burning higher up caused by infections, do not sing at all. Get yourself checked out medically first. It could be the first sign of a lesion on your vocal cords, your wake-up call about acid reflux, or even something more serious.

Several natural remedies can soothe a burning throat and help to clear bacterial infections without antibiotics.

- Slippery elm bark is recommended as "possibly effective" by the US National Library of Medicine (Collins, 2019). It can be found in a Chinese remedy which many voice actors swear, called Nin Jiom Pei Pa Koa throat syrup.

- Ginger and fresh lemon are excellent to soothe the burning caused by acid reflux. Ginger is a natural antibiotic, and it also helps to calm the digestive tract. Herbal tea with a slice of lemon and a few slivers of fresh ginger is refreshing and hydrating.
- The opera singer Jennifer Holloway believes in a concoction of ginger, honey, lemon, and turmeric. She peels, cuts, and boils a whole knob of ginger for about 15 minutes. Then she strains the liquid and adds the honey, lemon, and turmeric (Collins, 2019).
- Manuka honey has long been touted as a rich source of anti-microbial agents. It has now been shown as effective against multiple drug-resistant pathogens (Carter et al., 2016).
- In other studies, honey was also found to be an effective cough soother (Paul et al., 2007).
- Gargling with either a strong saline solution on its own or a saline solution with a quarter of a teaspoon of baking soda added can help to disinfect the throat.
- The bromelain found in pineapples can help break down mucus. Just be careful if you are prone to acid reflux.
- One or two drops at a time of oregano oil mixed with water or coconut oil can help fight a bacterial infection. Oregano contains carvacrol and thymol that act against bacteria and fungi.
- Some people believe in the antibiotic power of raw garlic and onion. Just make sure you won't be close to someone else the next day!
- A tea with fenugreek or marshmallow root can also be soothing and healing on a sore, inflamed throat.

## THE TONGUE, JAW, AND NECK

Tension in the tongue, jaw, and neck muscles can create unnecessary pain and stiffness that adversely affect your sound.

Watch yourself in a mirror for a while and note how you breathe and which muscles move.

Recite the lyrics of a song you are working on at a normal speech level while watching yourself. Do you see any excessive movement in your neck muscles? That could be indicative of bad posture and diction habits.

Ways of getting rid of the physical tension will be discussed in the section about physical workouts. It is, however, important that you identify the emotional causes of your tension.

Perhaps you have performance anxiety or a lack of confidence in your singing abilities? Do you worry too much about what others will think of your voice? Trust your vocal abilities and the exercises you do, and just enjoy your passion for singing. Stay within a range where you are comfortable and completely at ease until you feel more confident.

Do you suffer from the misconception that singing must be difficult because it's so different from talking? You could be trying too hard and complicated matters that are not so difficult, after all. This type of stress tends to be most noticeable in higher notes, where the tension in the vocal folds and pressure from the breath are at their peak. Inexperienced singers tighten their muscles in an effort to move up the musical scale.

If you have reached a basic skill level and your mind is right, your thoughts are relaxed, and you enjoy your singing, the physical component will be far easier, and much of it will come naturally, even when you are still fairly new at singing.

In the 18th century, Italian vocal coaches coined the phrase *si canta come si parla*. It means that you sing the same way you speak. Any attempts at complicated vocal acrobatics go against this adage and should be avoided to lessen stress.

A quick exercise to get rid of tongue tension is to simulate chewing with slightly parted lips. Next, you can hum a few bars while still doing the chewing motion.

If you suffer from excessive tension in your jaw, it might be that you clench your teeth without being aware of it. It could happen while concentrating on something or when you're asleep.

Make sure you're not thrusting your jaw forward and tensing your neck and the muscles below the jaw in the process. That will push the tongue back and elevate the larynx, resulting in a thin sound.

Keep your tongue, teeth, and gums healthy through regular brushing and flossing to avoid oral infections.

# THE IMPACT OF FOOD, DRINKS, AND MEDICATION

Any excessively spicy or acidic foods can irritate the throat enough that throat clearing goes into overdrive. The result will be swollen vocal folds that can't sing on pitch and a weaker sound.

If you frequently need to clear your throat, try swallowing instead. Substitute coughing for forceful exhalations when possible.

The irritating foods and too much alcohol can cause one of a singer's number one enemies: reflux.

## Acid Reflux

When stomach acid pushes back up through the esophagus due to the sphincter not closing properly, it causes a burning sensation commonly known as heartburn. Some people do not experience the feeling of heartburn, only the burned esophagus, and throat—that is called silent reflux. Silent reflux, also known as laryngopharyngeal reflux, usually creeps up on you at night while you sleep because your head is not elevated anymore.

The gastric acid mixes with saliva and causes a very sore throat, shortness of breath, a persistent feeling like there is a lump in the throat, and chest pain.

For a singer, acid reflux means a sudden struggle to reach higher pitches, a weak voice, and problems with correct breathing.

Chronic and severe acid reflux is known as gastroesophageal reflux disease (GERD).

The foods we eat, the drinks we consume, and the time of day we eat and drink will influence the severity of the reflux. If you totally can't live without some of the items on the list of things to avoid, consume them in moderation and not at night. If those foods and liquids remain in your stomach when you lie down to sleep, you're almost guaranteed to experience the reflux of acid through your esophagus.

Eating smaller and more frequent meals instead of fewer, large meals also benefits many sufferers of reflux and GERD.

Antacids relieve the burning sensation but don't heal the damaged esophagus. Overusing antacids can lead to constipation or diarrhea, headaches, nausea, and hypercalcemia (too much calcium in the blood).

## Foods to Avoid

The trans fats in fast food can aggravate acid reflux.

The general consensus among food experts is that certain types of food and drinks have to be avoided totally to ease reflux.

These include:

- High-fat foods such as French fries, onion rings, bacon, lard, full-fat dairy products, creamy sauces, creamy salad dressings, potato chips, greasy foods, and fatty cuts of meat.

- Fried foods.
- All citrus fruits, tomatoes, tomato products, and salsa.
- Chocolate.
- Garlic.
- Onions.
- Spicy foods such as chili.
- All kinds of pepper.
- Mint and all products made with it.
- Egg yolks.
- For some people, flour products such as bread also trigger reflux.
- All carbonated beverages.
- Coffee and tea.

## Foods to Eat

Avocados can be a delicious meal on their own.

Your aim to ease reflux symptoms is to consume foods that cause the least gastric acid to be produced during the digestive process.

The recommended list includes:

- High-fiber foods such as whole grains.
- All vegetables except those in the list of items to avoid.

- Non-citrus fruits, especially bananas and melons.
- Oatmeal.
- Ginger.
- Seafood and lean cuts of meat. Prepare them by grilling, baking, broiling, or poaching them.
- Egg whites.
- Healthy fats such as avocados, olives, walnuts, flaxseed, sesame oil, and sunflower oil.
- Still water.
- Herbal teas.

## Medications That Can Worsen Reflux

Don't neglect a cold or flu, but choose your remedies wisely.

Certain medications increase stomach acid or irritate the lining of the esophagus and should be avoided if possible. Do not, however, simply stop taking prescribed medications before speaking to your doctor.
They include:

- Antibiotics.
- Pain relievers such as aspirin and ibuprofen.
- Osteoporosis drugs that work by slowing down bone loss.

- Iron supplements.
- Potassium supplements.
- Heart medications containing quinidine.
- Cholinergic drugs that are commonly used to treat incontinence, chronic obstructive pulmonary disorder, and certain symptoms of Parkinson's disease.
- Tricyclic antidepressants.
- Some high blood pressure medications.
- Opioids such as codeine.
- Progesterone supplements.
- Tranquilizers.
- Medications containing theophylline that are used to treat asthma and other respiratory diseases.

# SMOKING AND SINGING

**Vaping is not better than regular smoking.**

It has been proven that smoking can wreak havoc on your vocal cords. Although some singers cultivate the raspy quality that comes with the "smoker's voice," the high price that your vocal instrument has to pay is not worth it.

Tobacco in any form dries out the vocal folds and irritates them. Vaping, unfortunately for the smokers among us, is no better. The vapor from e-cigarettes contains other potentially harmful substances besides nicotine, such as the flavoring chemical diacetyl.

Diacetyl can cause an irreversible lung disease known as obliterative bronchiolitis. The result is the narrowing down of the small airways in the lungs by scar tissue that forms when the body tries to heal the inflammation initially caused by the diacetyl.

The problem for singers is compounded by the fact that smoking aggravates reflux and GERD, leading to even more irritation of the throat and vocal cords.

It is a myth that staying silent while smoking will limit the damage. The smoke moves over the vocal folds, and the damage will occur, whether they are vibrating at that moment or not.

## Vocal Fold Damage

The vocal folds swell when they get irritated. That means their water content increases, which changes the pitch of the person's voice. That causes the gravelly character that distinguishes the voices of most smokers from non-smokers.

Swollen vocal cords are far more likely to develop lesions that will bleed and cause scar tissue. The result will be a permanent voice change and a sure loss of your higher range if any voice is left.

## Lung Capacity

Breathing well is essential for singing properly. Smoking reduces the capacity of the lungs to fill with air, and deep, correct breathing becomes difficult.

That, in turn, decreases the airflow over your vocal folds, leading to a loss of control in the voice.

## The Formation of Mucus

Our airways and lungs are kept clear of mucus by the cilia on the cells. Cilia are eyelash-like protuberances that stop unwanted substances and organisms from entering a cell.

A smoker's lung cilia get coated in tar and can't function properly anymore. They can't remove the phlegm as designed to, and mucus builds up.

The result is frequent coughing, especially just after waking up. The coughing causes the vocal folds to swell even more, and a vicious cycle starts.

In addition to the coughing, the folds themselves struggle to get rid of phlegm because the cilia can't protect them any longer.

# A PHYSICAL WORKOUT

Kickboxing is a good way to increase stamina.

Singing takes a lot of energy, both physically and emotionally. Exercise not only increases stamina and improves muscle tone, but it is also a much-needed way to get rid of the tension that builds up when preparing for and executing a performance. It is necessary to blow off the steam before moving on to the next project.

If you exercise on a day you will be performing, auditioning, or rehearsing, give yourself enough time to rest between your workout and the singing. The amount of rest time you need will depend on your fitness level.

You can exercise either indoors or outdoors. When going outdoors on a cold day, take care to protect your throat from the chilly air. Cold air dries out the vocal folds, and especially if it is performance day, you don't want that.

If jogging is your cup of tea, stay off urban roads until the air pollution is at its lowest.

Good types of sport to increase endurance are aerobic exercises such as swimming, martial arts, cycling, hiking, skating, or basketball.

If you can't do aerobics, try callanetics or Pilates. All of these will strengthen your core without overdoing it, which will make breathing difficult.

The breathing techniques taught in yoga can also benefit your singing tremendously.

Sports that could hamper your vocal development are power weight-lifting (it could cause incorrect posture focus), competitive long-distance and marathon running, professional ballet, and cheerleading.

## Let's Get Practical

While not every vocal student wants to become an opera singer, every type of singing performance is physically demanding. A typical pop concert requires just as much energy from the performers as a three-hour opera, if not more.

The American operatic soprano Kathryn Grumley starts warming up her voice every morning at nine. After a couple of vocal exercises, she's off to the gym for an aerobic workout before the rest of an eight-hour shift taken up by singing lessons, rehearsals, and performances.

Pop artist Rihanna has a 30-minute Pilates session and a five-kilometer run three to five times per week. She ends every workout with a strength routine of dumbbell lunges, squats, and reverse crunches.

Singer Shakira varies her workouts between dancing, playing tennis, and doing aerobic exercises in the gym.

## A Sample Core and Abdominal Routine

Strengthening the abdominal muscles and core can be one of the best things you can do for your singing career. Here are some sample exercises to help you get started.

Remember to start slow, especially if you don't have time for a full physical warmup.

Whereas many workout routines, especially from celebrities, focus on visible muscles and will change your appearance as quickly as possible, singers have to include the invisible muscles that help with breathing and support.

Crunches are widely touted as the best for developing abs. Still, if you neglect spinal flexion, rotation, stabilization, and extension, you will likely develop residual tension in your abs that will impede breathing.

### Spinal Flexion

A great exercise for spinal flexion that does not put any pressure on your back is the supine flexion.

- Lie on your back and bend your knees.
- Slowly lift your knees toward your chest. If you have a spinal injury or chronic back pain, lift only one knee at a time.
- Grab your knees with your hands and gently pull them even closer to your chest.
- Hold the position for a few moments and relax.
- If you have only a minute or two between rehearsals, do the exercise in a sitting position.

- Open your knees and bend down as far as possible.
- Try to put your palms flat on the floor without straining your back.
- If you can't reach the floor, just go down as low as you can. The idea is to keep your back muscles relaxed and use your abs to stay in position.
- If you feel up to it, you can grab hold of your ankles and give a gentle tug.
- The exercise can also be performed standing, which will target your hamstrings as well.

## Spinal Rotation

The lower back rotational stretch can release any tension from standing for long periods. It will provide a gentle core workout at the same time.

- Lie down on the floor or a yoga mat (any firm surface will do), bend your knees and keep your feet flat on the ground.
- Make sure both your shoulders are flat on the floor without pulling them back or straining any muscles in the upper body and neck.
- Roll both your knees over to one side in a gentle, controlled movement. Don't allow your legs to fall to the floor, jerking your back. Lower them slowly.
- Stay in the position for five to 10 seconds before returning your knees to the starting point.
- Repeat the exercise to the other side.
- Do two or three repetitions, or carry on until you feel the tension release.

If you know you'll be out, and on your feet for a whole day, it might be a good idea to get a medium-strength resistance band with handles and keep it in your bag. Whenever you have a break, you can anchor one handle of the resistance band around something heavy or hook it over a doorknob to take the rotation exercise up a notch.

- Stand at a right angle to the resistance band's handle with your feet slightly more than hip-width apart.
- Take the handle in both hands while still facing your body forward—your arms and shoulders will be turned in the direction of the band, while your trunk and legs will face forward.
- Pull the resistance band across your body as far as you can get it without straining unduly or causing any pain.

You can also rotate your back right there in your chair if there's no chance of doing the exercise lying down or standing.

- Sit with both feet flat on the floor.
- Place your interlaced hands behind your head, keeping your shoulders relaxed.
- Twist your torso to the right and hold the stretch for about 10 seconds.
- If you can't lift your arms high, you can simply put your left hand on your right knee to aid and stabilize the stretch.
- Repeat the exercise to the other side.

## Spinal Stabilization

The traditional plank exercise.

The classic exercise to stabilize the spine is known as the plank. It is used extensively in Pilates routines.

The point of the plank is that you have to keep most of your body in a straight line off the ground through muscle strength. A full plank is supported on the toes and forearms, while a partial plank is supported on the knees and forearms.

It is important when doing the plank to make sure you don't push your buttocks upward. Your back has to stay flat to create the required straight line.

Your shoulders should not be humped, and your chin should be kept tucked in to prevent neck strain.

- Lie down on your stomach on the floor or on a yoga mat with your elbows under your shoulders and your palms flat on the floor.
- Keep your forearms and hands on the floor while raising your body slowly into forming a straight line.
- If you're opting for a partial plank (easier for beginners), bend your knees and hook your ankles, one behind the other, for added support before you raise your trunk.
- Hold the position as long as you can.

Taking the plank a step further with a sideways position.

### Spinal Extension

Extension exercises have the opposite effect from flexions. It helps strengthen and stretch the rectus abdominis, the long muscle in the front of the body commonly called the six-pack and strengthens the lower back.

Although it might seem that you're just bending backward, it is important to use the right technique to avoid injury. No jerky movements are allowed, and the stretch should not be taken too far. It should not hurt.

- Lie on the floor or on a yoga mat with your legs stretched out behind you.
- Position your hands under your shoulders and relax your shoulders and neck.
- Raise your upper body only, supporting your hips on the floor.
- Hold the position for three seconds before lowering yourself again.
- Repeat the exercise three to five times.

### A Few Other Beneficial Exercises

One of the most important core muscles is the gluteus maximus or buttock muscles. The bridge exercise will strengthen these muscles.

- Lie on your back on the floor or yoga mat and bend your knees.
- Keep your feet hip-width apart and your hands flat on the floor by your sides.
- Raise your torso upward until it forms a straight line between the knees and the shoulders.
- Squeeze your buttocks for two to three seconds before lowering your body to the floor.
- Repeat five to 10 times.

Strong pelvic muscles are necessary for a strong core. Pelvic tilts will strengthen your lower back and benefit your diaphragm.

- Start in the same position as the bridge.
- Instead of raising your torso as in the bridge, just arch your lower back to push your stomach out.
- Hold the arch for five seconds.
- Flatten your lower back and imagine you're sucking your belly button now into the floor.
- Hold that position for five seconds too.
- Do at least ten repetitions.

## Simple Yoga for Singers

Besides the breath control taught in yoga, the stretches can also immensely benefit a singer's posture and stamina.

The postures, called asanas, can be combined with positive affirmations and visualizations to enhance their effect.

### Cat-Cow Pose

The cat-cow posture is a time-honored asana for strength, relaxation, and flexibility. It is simple and quick to do.

- Get down on your hands and knees.
- Keep your knees hip-width apart.
- Imagine pulling your belly button up to your spine by arching your back as a cat would.
- Hold the position for a moment or two before allowing your abdomen to sag toward the floor, hollowing your back. That is the cow part of the posture.
- Relax after a couple of seconds and repeat the stretch.

### Halfway Lift/Straight Back Pose

A relaxed neck and shoulders equal a relaxed larynx, which is good news for a singer. The asana mainly works on the trapezius muscle that stretches over most of the upper back and counters the effects of sitting all day.

- Stand in a forward bend, letting your arms and hands dangle toward the floor.
- If you are flexible enough to touch your hands to the floor, you can do so.
- Bend your knees and draw your hips back. Get the feeling that your spine is elongating.
- Lift your hips high enough to feel your back muscles engaging but without straining them.
- Support your fingertips on your shins.
- Keep your head and neck in a straight line with your back and direct your gaze downward.
- To add a degree of difficulty, you can extend your arms backward for a few seconds and then forward again like Superman while holding your back straight and your knees bent.

### Pigeon Pose

This pose opens up the hips and gives a feeling that the column of air you breathe fills your whole torso. It helps when you are struggling to reach some high notes because it enhances breathing.

- Start on all fours with your hands slightly in front of your shoulders and your knees below your hips.
- Slide your right knee forward carefully until your knee is outside your right wrist. Slide your right foot forward in the same motion to rest in front of your left knee, with the outside of your right knee resting on the floor.

- Move your left leg backward slowly and carefully. Take it slow and stop if it hurts. Do not injure yourself if you are not flexible yet.
- Lower your left thigh as close to the floor as you can while keeping a straight leg.
- Allow the outside of your right buttock to rest on the floor.
- Make sure your right heel is in front of your left hip and support yourself on your hands. Keep your arms straight.
- Roll your left hip joint forward toward your right heel and square your pelvic area as much as possible.
- Move your hands to your sides, so your fingertips rest on the floor while pushing your torso upright.
- Keep your gaze forward.
- Hold the position for as long as you are comfortable or for about ten seconds before relaxing.
- Repeat the pose on the other side.

## Mountain Pose

As we have seen in the earlier discussions about the right posture for singing, it is important how you stand when you sing.

The mountain pose is an active, elongating standing position through which unnecessary tension can be released before you sing the first note.

- Stand facing forward and with your feet parallel to each other, a few inches apart.
- Keep your arms by your sides and your hands open and relaxed, palms facing in- or forward.
- Lift and spread your toes before putting them down again to balance your weight evenly.
- Lift your breastbone toward the ceiling without pushing out any of your lower ribs.

- Relax your shoulders and allow your shoulder blades to draw toward each other, widening your collar bones and moving your shoulders away from your ears.
- Position your head, so your crown is directly above your pelvis.
- Your chin should be parallel to the floor, your throat and jaw relaxed, and your tongue flat and wide on the floor of your mouth.
- Breathe deeply from your diaphragm until you feel ready to sing the first note with conviction and power.

## Winding Down

A stability ball and a resistance band on a yoga mat.

After your invigorating workout, you should give your body a chance to cool down just like your voice needs. Your body temperature, blood pressure, and heart rate have to return to normal before carrying on with your everyday activities.

Gentle stretches are all that's needed.

- If you have a big stability ball, you can lie down over it on your back and reach over your head to touch your hands to the floor while breathing deeply.

- The legs-against-the-wall position is a great way to calm the heart rate and allow any accumulated tension to flow away. Lie down on a yoga mat next to a wall or lie on your bed with your feet facing the headboard. Move your hips as close to the wall as you can and walk your legs up the wall until your body is in an L-shape. Breathe calmly and deeply and allow your thoughts to wander for at least five minutes.

# IN SUMMARY

Don't worry if you feel your head is spinning after this chapter. This handy summary will keep all the most important points together for you!

- Always try to avoid using your voice to the point of going hoarse.
- Don't try to hold a lengthy conversation in noisy places; it puts great strain on the vocal folds.
- Whispering is just as bad for your vocal cords in terms of strain.
- Rest your voice when you are sick.
- Keep your surroundings humid.
- Keep yourself hydrated with water at room temperature or herbal teas.
- NEVER skip your warmup.
- Keep as quiet as possible after a strenuous vocal day, except for a short cooling routine, to give your voice a chance to recuperate.
- Practice your good breathing techniques while you talk as well.
- Don't cradle your phone between your head and shoulder while talking to someone. That causes much muscle tension.
- Use a microphone when needed.
- Don't be shy to get professional help if you suspect your vocal folds have developed problems.
- Avoid acid-causing foods and drinks as much as possible.

- Don't ignore acid reflux and GERD in the hope that you will escape damage and it will go away on its own—change your diet and lifestyle, and get medical attention if needed.
- Stop smoking.
- Don't neglect your physical workout and relaxation exercises.

# SINGING AFTER 50

Advancing age does not spare any part of our existence from changes, and our voices are no exception. However, that does not mean that you have to accept a limit to your singing career just because you turn 50 or 60.

Your good habits over the years, combined with a couple of extra things once you reach more senior age, can ensure you can keep singing as long as you want. After all, the saying among singers is, "We don't stop singing because we grow old. We grow old because we stop singing."

Just to inspire you, here are the names of a couple of singers who were 75 years or older at the beginning of 2021 and are still recording and touring:

- Willie Nelson, 87.
- Dionne Warwick, 80.
- Paul McCartney, 78.
- Ringo Starr, 80.
- Loretta Lynn, 88.
- Bob Dylan, 79.
- In the Rolling Stones, all of the group members are over 70.
- Barbra Streisand, 78.

- Nana Mouskouri, 86.
- Dolly Parton, 75.

Need I say more to get you into good vocal habits today?

# WHY DO OUR VOICES CHANGE?

As we age, our vocal folds weaken. In females, changes in the hormonal balance result in an increase in density in the vocal cords. Thicker vocal cords mean a lower female voice. This change starts right after menopause when estrogen production decreases.

In addition to the increase in density, the female larynx also sinks a bit lower in the throat after menopause due to changes in muscle tone.

Their decreased production of testosterone precipitates the vocal changes for men. That raises their general voice pitch somewhat but, unfortunately, does not raise their previously highest note as well.

In some people, part of the cartilage around the larynx calcifies as they get older. That makes them harder, and high pitches become difficult to reach due to the loss of flexibility. The stiffness is exacerbated by a history of acid reflux and smoking.

The vocal folds themselves, being muscles, start to dry out, and they can atrophy in extreme cases.

If your overall fitness level is declining, chronic fatigue could cause a tremor that will only be noticeable to other people.

The respiratory system, as well as the supporting abdominal and rib muscles, weaken without regular exercise. This can be heard in an aging singer's wobble that sounds like an exaggerated vibrato but is so violent that the singer goes off the pitch without noticing it.

If you develop sudden, persistent hoarseness or faintness in the voice that lasts for more than two weeks, it would be prudent to talk to a medical professional. Hoarseness and other voice changes can be early symptoms of Parkinson's disease and Alzheimer's disease.

Voice changes slip in gradually, and you may not notice them for a while. That is where a trusted vocal coach can be invaluable, not only to make you aware of the changes but to help you work through them and adapt your exercise routines.

# TIPS TO KEEP THE MELODY GOING

Without repeating the whole ebook you have been reading so far, let's just start by saying you should never stop practicing, always keep your breathing techniques tip-top, and never sing without warming your voice up first.

When you find your breath control is getting more difficult, concentrate on exercises that force you to exhale in a controlled way. An example would be to inhale on four counts, hold your breath for two counts, and exhale on an 's' sound for as long as you can sustain it.

When preparing for a concert or other big event, pace your singing more deliberately than when you were younger. You don't have to force your voice through the same number of hours' practice as before, but that probably means you will have to start rehearsing earlier.

Adequate hydration gets even more important as we age. Take care of your eating habits to avoid acid reflux. If you're still smoking, it is becoming crucial now to stop.

Don't skip physical workouts and concentrate on flexibility and core strength. Resistance bands are excellent partners on this journey.

Above all, don't beat yourself up about the changes you feel and hear in your voice. Aging is a privilege many don't get to experience. Enlist the help of a speech therapist with specialized training in singing voices if necessary. Botox and other filler injections for the vocal folds are also available from reputable ear, nose, and throat specialists.

Embrace your changes with enthusiasm and reinvent yourself!

# OLDER MALE SINGERS

As the vocal folds in men become thinner and stiffer after middle age, the general pitch of their voices rises.

The edges of the folds become ragged instead of straight, and the folds don't close as tightly as they used to. The gap between them lets air escape, and the sound they produce becomes breathy and weak. The condition is known as presbylarynx, or bowling vocal cords, due to the spindle shape of the opening.

Presbylarynx makes the voice unstable, and unexpected switches to falsetto, similar to yodeling, may occur when the volume increases.

Even with the best precautions, changes will happen and can be upsetting. Voice therapy as soon as possible has a good prognosis of helping you keep the quality of your voice steady for longer.

# THE AGING FEMALE SINGER

Whereas the vocal folds in males get thinner with age, the opposite happens in females. The folds become slightly swollen due to hormonal changes.

The number of glands that supply mucus to keep them moist diminishes while the mucus itself becomes thicker and harder to clear.

All of this adds up to a slightly lower and sometimes hoarse and breathy voice quality if left unchecked.

Middle age and menopause are by far not the end of the road for female singers, though. The renowned British teacher of mature female voices, Becky Moseley-Morgan, believes targeting the right muscles will stop the decline and preserve the quality of the voice, both in terms of range and volume (iSingmag, 2019).

Moseley-Morgan focuses on breathing and register changes and gives her students homework for at least 20 minutes every other day.

According to Dr. Patti Peterson of the North American choral movement GALA Choruses, the head voice should get particular attention. It tends to decline first because of the lower seat of the larynx (Peterson, 2014).

Peterson recommends the Stemple exercises that voice therapist Joseph Stemple developed from Kentucky University. They work on all the registers.

## The Stemple Exercises

According to Peterson, it is important to do these exercises very softly. Singing softly is more difficult than singing loudly, and it will give the vocal apparatus a better workout.

Stemple's exercises target the laryngeal muscles in terms of balance, tone, stamina, and strength. They can be compared to physical therapy for the vocal cords.

Be on the lookout for any breaks in quality and breathiness while you perform them. Do each exercise twice in a row and perform the full set of exercises twice a day.

- The first exercise: Sustain an 'i' vowel as long as possible on F3 for males and F4 for females. Make sure the tone is soft but not breathy; bright and forward, not nasal.
- The second exercise: Form a small 'o' with almost closed lips and glide from the lowest note you can reach to the highest. Remember that the sound must be soft, and your voice should not be strained. Don't stop if your voice breaks at any point. If the sound breaks off before you're at the top note, continue using your vocal folds as if you are producing sound. This exercise will promote the slow and steady engagement of the muscles that produce the head voice.
- The third exercise: Reverse the second exercise using the same vowel and mouth position. This time, gliding down the scale at very low volume targets the muscles that produce the chest voice.

- The fourth exercise: Start on C3 for men and C4 for women with the vowel 'o.' Move up to D, E, F, and G, all on one breath. Repeat the sequence as long as you can in the same breath. When your air starts to run out, you should take care not to use your throat to produce the sound. Let your abdominal muscles take over to support your vocal folds.

# CONCLUSION

Now that the secret to becoming a great singer isn't a secret to you, go on and explore your talent! You received your voice for a reason, and you may win a million hearts sooner than you think.

All you need is to decide you're going to do it and then take the first step in your vocal development.

This book has given you the basic knowledge you need to get started, and what you're going to do with it is up to you.

The world can be your stage—go for it!

## REQUEST FOR A REVIEW

If the information in this book has opened up the world of singing for you and inspired you to take action, please leave a positive review on Amazon so others can make the same breakthroughs.

# A SINGER'S GLOSSARY

This is a brief glossary of some important terms used in this ebook for quick reference.

| A Capella | Singing without accompaniment. |
|---|---|
| Alto | The low female voice part in a choir; often used interchangeably with contralto. |
| Baritone | The middle male voice type. |
| Bass | The lowest male voice type. |
| Contralto | The lowest female voice type. |
| Diaphragm | A dome-shaped muscle running under the ribs and lungs to separate the chest and abdominal cavities from each other. The diaphragm is essential for breathing. |
| Diction | The clear and correct pronunciation of words. |
| Dynamics | The changes in tempo and volume in a song. |
| Falsetto | The highest part of the male register. |
| Flat | To sing under the correct pitch. |
| Larynx | The voice box that sits at the top of the neck. |
| Legato | Notes that are sung smoothly and connectedly. |
| Mezzo-Soprano | The middle female voice type. |

| | |
|---|---|
| Nodules/Nodes | Non-malignant bumps that can form on the vocal folds. |
| Phrasing | The timing of the points where breaths are taken between words to form coherent and pleasing sections sung on one breath. |
| Pitch | The frequency of a sound, high, medium, or low. |
| Range | The notes a person can sing comfortably. |
| Register | The range of tones produced by a particular vibration pattern of the vocal folds and other body parts. |
| Resonance | The amplification of sound in different parts of the body. |
| Scale | A set of musical notes following each other according to pitch and musical rules. |
| Sharp | To sing above the correct pitch. |
| Soft palate/velum | The soft tissue at the back of the mouth. |
| Soprano | The highest female voice type. |
| Staccato | The opposite of legato; each note is sung on its own in a short burst of sound. |
| Tenor | The highest male voice type. |
| Tone | The timbre or color of a note. |
| Vibrato | The vibrating quality of a sound. |
| Vocal cords/folds | The two muscular folds with vibrating tissue in the throat that produce sound. |

# REFERENCES

Cadman, B. (2020, January 24). *10 exercises to strengthen the lower back.* Www.medicalnewstoday.com. https://www.medicalnewstoday.com/ articles/323204

Carter, D. A., Blair, S. E., Cokcetin, N. N., Bouzo, D., Brooks, P., Schothauer, R., & Harry, E. J. (2016). Therapeutic manuka honey: No longer so alternative. *Frontiers in Microbiology, 7.* https://doi. org/10.3389/fmicb.2016.00569

Chapman, A. (2021, July 8). *How to find your vocal range.* WikiHow. https://www.wikihow.com/Find-Your-Vocal-Range

Ciccarelli, S. (2009, July 2). *Dangers of whispering and how it affects your voice.* Voices. https://www.voices.com/blog/ the_dangers_of_whispering_for_your_voice/

City Academy. (2016, February 3). *How to find your voice type.* City Academy. https://www.city-academy.com/news/how-to-find-your-voice-type/

Cleveland Clinic. (2021). *Diaphragm: Hiatal hernia, diaphragmatic breathing, what is the diaphragm.* Cleveland Clinic. https://my.cleveland-clinic.org/health/body/21578-diaphragm

Collins, S. (2019, January 2). *Sore throat soothers: Secrets of the voice pros.* WebMD. https://www.webmd.com/cold-and-flu/news/20190103/ secrets-of-the-voice-pros-sore-throat-soothers

Columbia University Irving Medical Center. (2017, February 9). *Vocal fold cancer.* Department of Otolaryngology Head and Neck Surgery. https://www.entcolumbia.org/health-library/vocal-fold-cancer

Copadis, A. (2017, July 30). *What's my voice type? Your guide to defining your voice.* VoicesInc.org. https://www.voicesinc.org/voice-types/

Edwards, M. (2015, August 13). *Vocal damage in classical singers: It's not just pop singers that get hurt.* Matt Edwards. https://edwardsvoice. wordpress.com/2015/08/13/vocal-damage-in-classical-singers-its-not-just-pop-singers-that-get-hurt/

Ewer, G. (2020, June 10). *5 tips for analyzing songs, and the benefits you'll see with your own songwriting.* The Essential Secrets of Songwriting. https://www.secretsofsongwriting.com/2020/06/10/5-tips-for-analy zing-songs-and-the-benefits-youll-see-with-your-own-songwriting/

Friedlander, C. (2014, October 31). *Singing & abdominal exercise.* The Liberated Voice. https://www.claudiafriedlander.com/ the-liberated-voice/2014/10/abs.html

G, J. (2012, July 18). *A quick primer on the mechanics of speech.* Speech Buddies Blog: Speech, Language & Pronunciation Guides. https:// www.speechbuddy.com/blog/language-development/a-quick-p rimer-on-the-mechanics-of-speech/

Gemtracks. (2021, August 10). *10+ famous bass singers in the world.* Gemtracks Beats. https://www.gemtracks.com/guides/view. php?title=famous-bass-singers-in-the-world&id=890

George's Opera World. (2020, December 5). *Luciano Pavarotti - vocalizing on "passaggio". Vocal warm-up for tenors.* Www.youtube.com. https:// www.youtube.com/watch?v=kuiqJ5IeXsA

Harmonic Sounds. (2021). *Overtone singing: The essence of harmony.* Harmonic Sounds Association of Sound Therapy. https://harmon-icsounds.com/sound-healing/overtone-singing/

Harmonic Voices. (2013). *Amazing Grace with overtone singing by Nestor Kornblum.* Www.youtube.com. https://www.youtube.com/ watch?v=nPu9XMMY1Y8

Harris, S. (2012). *The voice & aging.* Britishvoiceassociation.org.uk. https:// www.britishvoiceassociation.org.uk/voicecare_the-voice-and-ageing.htm

Henny, J. (2021, January 21). *How the vocal cords work for singing.* John Henny Vocal Studio. https://johnhenny.com/how-the-vocal-cord s-work-for-singing/

iSingmag. (2019, October 22). *Mature female singers: Teaching tips and myths*. Www.isingmag.com. https://www.isingmag.com/mature-female-singers-teaching-tips-and-myths/

Jonithm. (2015, March 26). *Let's talk Fachs-the dramatic mezzo*. TalesofTessitura. https://talesoftessitura.wordpress.com/2015/03/26/lets-talk-fachs-the-dramatic-mezzo/

Kaur Dhillon, V. (2021). *Vocal cord disorders*. Www.hopkinsmedicine.org. https://www.hopkinsmedicine.org/health/conditions-and-diseases/vocal-cord-disorders

Kettler, S. (2020, October 15). *Julie Andrews had surgery to fix a "weak spot" on her vocal cords and lost her singing voice*. Biography. https://www.biography.com/news/julie-andrews-vocal-cord-surgery-lost-voice

Koopman, J. (2019). *A brief history of singing*. Lawrence.edu. https://www2.lawrence.edu/fast/KOOPMAJO/antiquity.html

Kubala, J. (2020, June 24). *The 20 best foods for lung health*. Healthline. https://www.healthline.com/nutrition/lung-cleansing-foods#20.-Cocoa

Madell, R. (2021, September 10). *Foods to avoid with acid reflux and GERD*. Healthline. https://www.healthline.com/health/gerd/foods-to-avoid#other-things

Mayo Clinic Staff. (2021, January 14). *Throat cancer - symptoms and causes*. Mayo Clinic. https://www.mayoclinic.org/diseases-conditions/throat-cancer/symptoms-causes/syc-20366462

Medina, J. (2021, July). *Alessandro Moreschi sings Ave Maria (no scratch)*. Www.youtube.com. https://www.youtube.com/watch?v=KLjvfqnD0ws

Music Services, Inc. (2021). *Do I need permission to create an arrangement or use an arrangement of a public domain work?* Musicservices.org. https://musicservices.org/node/5089#:~:text=In%20the%20United%20States%2C%20works

Musicnotes Now. (2019, February 6). *Expand your vocal range with these 10 simple tips*. Musicnotes Now. https://www.musicnotes.com/now/tips/expand-your-vocal-range-with-these-10-simple-tips/

Myers, E. (1996, December 28). *Contraltos*. Www.metguild.org. https://www.metguild.org/operanews/_archive/122896/contraltos.122896.html

National Cancer Institute. (2019). *Laryngeal cancer treatment.* National Cancer Institute; Cancer.gov. https://www.cancer.gov/types/head-and-neck/patient/adult/laryngeal-treatment-pdq

National Center for Voice and Speech. (2021). *Vocal ring, or the singer's formant.* Ncvs.org. http://www.ncvs.org/ncvs/tutorials/voiceprod/tutorial/singer.html

NDR Elbphilharmonie Orchester. (2021, May 10). *Maria Callas singt: "O don fatale" aus Verdis Don Carlo.* Www.youtube.com. https://www.youtube.com/watch?v=MvIc8-Ni4QM

O'Connor, K. (2020a). *Anatomy of the voice.* SingWise. https://www.singwise.com/articles/anatomy-of-the-voice

O'Connor, K. (2020b). *Correct breathing and "support" for singing.* SingWise. https://www.singwise.com/articles/correct-breathing-and-support-for-singing

O'Connor, K. (2020c). *How to eliminate register breaks (and develop evenness of scale).* SingWise. https://www.singwise.com/articles/how-to-eliminate-register-breaks-and-develop-evenness-of-scale

O'Connor, K. (2020d). *Singing with an "open throat": Vocal tract shaping.* SingWise. https://www.singwise.com/articles/singing-with-an-open-throat-vocal-tract-shaping

O'Connor, K. (2020e). *Understanding vocal range, vocal registers, and voice type: A glossary of vocal terms.* SingWise. https://www.singwise.com/articles/understanding-vocal-range-vocal-registers-and-voice-type-a-glossary-of-vocal-terms

O'Connor, K. (2020f). *Vibrato: What it is and how to develop It.* SingWise. https://www.singwise.com/articles/vibrato-what-it-is-and-how-to-develop-it

Open Music Theory. (n.d.). *Pitches and octave designations.* Open Music Theory. http://openmusictheory.com/pitches.html

Oren, L. (2020, January 5). *7 yoga poses that will improve your singing.* YogiApproved™. https://www.yogiapproved.com/yoga/how-to-improve-your-singing/

Paul, I. M., Beiler, J., McMonagle, A., Shaffer, M. L., Duda, L., & Berlin, C. M. (2007). Effect of honey, dextromethorphan, and no treatment on nocturnal cough and sleep quality for coughing children and their parents. *Archives of Pediatrics & Adolescent Medicine, 161*(12), 1140–1146. https://doi.org/10.1001/archpedi.161.12.1140

Peterson, Dr. P. (2014). *Practical remedies for the aging female voice.* Https://Galachoruses.org/. https://galachoruses.org/resource-center/singers/aging-voice/practical-remedies-for-the-aging-female-voice/

Picco, M. F. (2020, January 22). *GERD: Can certain medications make it worse?* Mayo Clinic. https://www.mayoclinic.org/diseases-conditions/gerd/expert-answers/heartburn-gerd/faq-20058535

Ramsey, M. (2017, August 1). *How to expand your vocal range with 3 easy exercises.* Ramsey Voice Studio. https://ramseyvoice.com/expand-vocal-range/

Robinson, I. (2021). *4 diaphragmatic breathing exercises for the beginner singer.* Jabberdi.com. https://jabberdi.com/7723/4-diaphragmatic-breathing-exercises-beginner-singer

Rory PQ. (2020, April 26). *10 best vocal warm-ups that will improve your singing.* Icon Collective College of Music. https://iconcollective.edu/best-vocal-warm-ups/

Sage Music. (2015, January 28). *Improving your singing voice part 1: Singing posture.* Sage Music | Piano, Voice, Guitar Lessons & More. https://www.sagemusic.co/improving-singing-voice-part-1-singing-posture/

Sanders, G. M. (2019, March 1). *Cardio workouts help this opera singer hit the high notes.* Austin Woman Magazine. https://atxwoman.com/opera-singer-kathryn-grumley-shares-workout-routine/

Santos-Longhurst, A. (2018, July 30). *Diaphragm overview.* Healthline; Healthline Media. https://www.healthline.com/human-body-maps/diaphragm#conditions

Sears, B. (2021, March 19). *3 exercises to do (in order) to properly progress low back flexion.* Verywell Health. https://www.verywellhealth.com/low-back-flexion-exercise-p2-2696216

Spohr, M. (2021, January 20). *16 legendary musicians over 75 who are still absolutely amazing.* BuzzFeed. https://www.buzzfeed.com/mikespohr/oldest-musicians-still-performing

Story, C. M., & Gotter, A. (2017, March 29). *12 natural remedies for sore throats*. Healthline. https://www.healthline.com/health/cold-flu/sore-throat-natural-remedies

Tobacco-Free Life. (2016). *Smoking and singing–how smoking affects your singing voice*. Tobacco-Free Life. https://tobaccofreelife.org/resources/smoking-singing/

Weill Cornell Sean Parker Institute for the Voice. (2016). Normal Phonation [YouTube Video]. In *YouTube*. https://www.youtube.com/watch?v=g4JBeKvFhz8

Weill Cornell Sean Parker Institute for the Voice. (2019). *Normal voice function*. Cornell.edu; Weill Cornell Medicine. https://voice.weill.cornell.edu/voice-evaluation/normal-voice-function

Whitten, S. (2018, April 8). *The importance of core training for singers*. Sarah Whitten Voice & Yoga. https://sarahwhitten.com/blog/the-importance-of-core-training-for-singers/

Woodhull, M. (2018). *Best sports for singers to work out and stay in shape*. Singingforaliving.com. https://www.singingforaliving.com/articles/sports-tips-for-singers/

# IMAGES

Alê, A. (2017). A cross-section showing how the tongue is anchored to the voice box. In *Pixabay*. https://pixabay.com/illustrations/the-larynx-the-pharynx-anatomy-2381980/

Art Core Studios. (2016). A stability ball and a resistance band on a yoga mat. In *Pixabay*. https://pixabay.com/photos/workout-ball-pilates-fitness-gym-1931107/

Buissinne, S. (2015a). Avocados can be a delicious meal on their own. In *Pixabay*. https://pixabay.com/photos/avocado-salad-fresh-food-829092/

Buissinne, S. (2015b). Don't neglect a cold or flu but choose your remedies wisely. In *Pixabay*. https://pixabay.com/photos/flu-influenza-cold-virus-sick-1006045/

Clicker-Free-Vector-Images. (2012). A detailed diagram showing the airways and diaphragm. In *Pixabay*. https://pixabay.com/vectors/health-medicine-anatomy-lung-41508/

Digital Photo & Design. (2016). Anyone can sing. In *Pixabay*. https://pixabay.com/photos/prairie-dog-singing-musical-rodent-1470659/

Everding, B. (2013). Choose your mouth opening according to the pitch you're singing at and the vowel you are forming. In *Pixabay*. https://pixabay.com/photos/singer-karaoke-girl-woman-to-sing-84874/

Free-Photos. (2016). Enthusiasm is a key ingredient in good singing. In *Pixabay*. https://pixabay.com/photos/microphone-boy-studio-screaming-1209816/

Haiberliu. (2017). Vaping is not better than regular smoking. In *Pixabay*. https://pixabay.com/photos/beauty-electronic-cigarette-smoke-2843930/

Janeb13. (2016). Kickboxing is a good way to increase stamina. In *Pixabay*. https://pixabay.com/photos/kickboxing-class-sports-hall-1178261/

Lee, Y. (2017). Tuning forks are good demonstrations of vibration and resonance-producing sound. In *Pixabay*. https://pixabay.com/photos/crystal-resonance-sound-2435411/

Making Music Fun. (2021). A simple rendition of Amazing Grace. In *Making Music Fun*. https://www.makingmusicfun.net/htm/f_print-it_free_printable_sheet_music/amazing-grace-easy-piano.php

No-longer-here. (2013). Piano keyboard. In *Pixabay*. https://pixabay.com/illustrations/piano-keyboard-piano-keyboard-black-163725/

RitaE. (2018). The trans fats in fast food can aggravate acid reflux. In *Pixabay*. https://pixabay.com/photos/burger-hamburger-bbq-food-3442227/

Serero, D. (2020). Baritone David Serero. In *Pixabay*. https://pixabay.com/photos/david-serero-opera-singer-actor-5142999/

Stocksnap. (2017). The traditional plank exercise. In *Pixabay*. https://pixabay.com/photos/people-woman-yoga-mat-meditation-2557452/

Wells, H. (2016). Taking the plank a step further with a sideways position. In *Pixabay*. https://pixabay.com/photos/plank-fitness-muscular-exercising-1327256/

Wikimediaimages. (2015). A scene from Rossini's opera The Barber of Seville in the Dupage Theater. In *Pixabay*. https://pixabay.com/photos/barber-seville-opera-performance-895148/

willywonka070. (2016). Drinking water is a singer's best way to stay hydrated. In *Pixabay*. https://pixabay.com/photos/refreshing-cool-water-hydrate-1406276/

Wolter, T. (2019). Whispering puts much strain on the voice. In *Pixabay*. https://pixabay.com/photos/ear-mouth-nose-face-head-voices-3971050/

Made in United States
Orlando, FL
22 May 2023

33355432R00083